THE ART OF FOCUS

3 EASY STEPS TO BUILD A LIFE YOU LOVE AND CONTROL YOUR TIME

CURTIS MCHALE

HAZEL ST PRESS

978-1-7753364-2-6 ISBN (Hardcover Print Edition)

978-1-7753364-3-3 ISBN (Paperback Print Edition)

978-1-7753364-4-0 ISBN (Electronic Edition)

All photographs by Curtis McHale unless otherwise noted.

First printing August 2018

Published by Hazel Street Press

PO Box 2207 Stn Main

Chilliwack, BC

V2R 1A6

Canada

Visit: https://curtismchale.ca

❀ Created with Vellum

CONTENTS

GET THE AUDIOBOOK AND WORKBOOK FOR FREE!

Just to say thanks for purchasing this book I want to give you two things for free.

To download go to:

https://curtismchale.ca/recommends/finding-focus-audio

If you sign for the email list as well you can get the first video module in my 8 Week Business BootCamp for free. The first module goes with Part I of this book and I know some people love video.

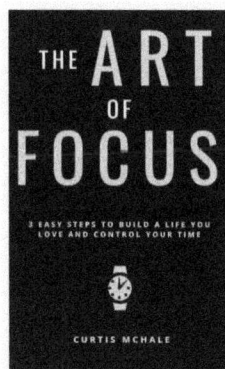

INTRODUCTION

If you've read anything on productivity and achieving your dreams, you've probably heard that you should follow your passion. You've probably also been told that you need to focus on a single thing with everything you have because it's in this focus that people see results.

Here is a quote from The One Thing to show you what I'm talking about:

"If disproportionate results come from one activity, then you must give that one activity disproportionate time. - The ONE Thing

That's easy to say for authors, coaches or other business people quoting this phrase about focus. More than likely, they have an accompanying $4,000 course they want to sell to teach you "how to focus" or "how to fund your single thing". They already have it "made".

In contrast, you're looking at the bank account and need to pay bills. This is something that your passion is not doing currently. It's still just a passion project, an idea. It hasn't caught on yet, and you're not sure that it ever will.

This book is for those of us that want to work on something we love. It's for those of us that want to build a schedule that lets them focus so they can produce enormous value in a regular day. It's for those of us that are tired of the "follow your passion" rhetoric; we want something concrete to use in our lives today.

I sat in the same spot as you do. I'd read books and listened to podcasts. I kept hearing that I should follow my passion. That all I had to do was focus on the stuff I cared about and I'd build a tribe that would love me for me. Then the money would follow like some torrential dam being released.

I spent a whole year doing this. Focusing on coaching and writing and reading. Sharing information and barely doing any web development because it wasn't something I was passionate about anymore.

I'm lucky I have a supportive wife, because I more than halved our income. Like Linus waiting for The Great Pumpkin, I kept trucking along waiting on the universe to notice my earnestness. I realized it was a sham, so I changed. This book will teach you the systems I implemented that produced actual results.

By not only looking at my passion and hoping that some benevolent mythical being would take care of the rest, I managed to turn it around.

This book is divided into three parts to walk you through how I made a change that mattered in my business.

Part I is going to look at how you can generate lots of ideas of things that might work. We're going to take all those ideas through a set of filters that are specific to you so that you don't build a business you end up hating. We're also going to look at how we test these ideas in the market before you start focusing on the one or two that have the most promise.

Part II is all about how you get serious about your focus so that you can have time to work on the things that you want to focus on. I believe that if you build a business with lots of income but ruin your relationships then you've failed. It's no good to have a bunch of money and be a terrible spouse or parent. Part II will help you negotiate this delicate balance by maximizing your creative time.

In Part III, we'll dive deep in to how you can test your final few ideas to see which one will get the most traction. These tests will help you determine which idea to focus on as the income is proof of demand for what you're offering. We'll plan a transition from whatever you're doing now in to what you want to do. I'll walk you through what it takes to get your spouse/partner on board so that you're not fighting with the business at the same time as having an uphill battle at home. Part III ends with a fairly deep discussion about dealing with the dark times that come when you're trying to launch a new idea.

Here's my Big Promise to you: If you're willing to put in the work, by the time you're done this book you'll have a path forward that is starting to show some fruit in the market. You'll have a system you can use again and again to see which ideas you should be pursuing in your life and business.

If you're not seeing this, then email me at curtis@curtismchale.ca and I'll hop on the phone for FREE for a strategy session to see where you're getting stuck.

Can you wait to read this book? Sure you can. If you're happy with the status quo you've got now, then don't read the book. If you're happy with your income, and your success, then go find something else to read.

If you're ready to make a change.

If you're ready to start working on something you care about that brings value to your customers.

If you're ready to spend more time with those you love without feeling like you're shortchanging your work...then it's time to read this book.

This system has been proven to work with my coaching students. I've used it over and over and refined it as I've helped people build a life that mattered to them.

It's time to take control of your life. It's time to build something that matters that doesn't take every hour of every day. It's time to start being that parent and spouse you always dreamed you'd be.

1

DEBUNKING SOME MYTHS

The first myth I want to debunk is that you should just follow your passion. This is another one of the things that seem so easy to say for some coach/guru to say in their presentation at a conference. It's totally different when you're trying to pay bills.

Your heart warming passion doesn't pay bills. Your landlord doesn't care that you are passionate about your work. They want money.

Your kids can't eat or wear your passion.

So, let's at least make passion take a step back. We want to enjoy what we do but there is something we need to look at first because you can find passion in almost everything you do, if you have purpose.

Second, let's be honest here with how hard this journey is. It's unlikely that your first idea will be the right one. It's unlikely that your second kick at the can is going to be the one that wins you all that life can give you.

It may be your 568th that wins. If you think that you'll read this book and then win tomorrow, you're fooling yourself. You should ask for a refund.

This book will help you find your focus and plan better so you have time to make that focus work for you. It's up to you to try things. It's going to be up to you to test your ideas and keep coming at it as you see things that work until you find something that others find valuable and that you enjoy doing.

PART I: PURPOSE MEETS PASSION

1

PURPOSE MEETS PASSION

I f you hate Monday and look forward to Friday, it's time to find something new. This often happens because you have no idea where you want to go. You're like some leaf on the wind, getting blown from here to there as the world wants to move you.

That's a terrible plan, but I've got a better one for you. By the end of this chapter you'll have an ideal plan for the life you want to build so that you can filter any new ideas and work to make sure they're taking you in the right direction.

Forget Passion, Establish Your Purpose

> Some people pursue passion in navigating their careers, but they also manage to connect this passion with a clear sense of purpose on the job—they contribute, serve others, make a difference. They have matched passion with purpose. - Great at Work

Many people have talked about your purpose. Some call it your why, or whatever word they want to use to enhance their intellectual property and sell you something.

It's easy to understand why so many are tired of hearing about purpose, as every coach and consultant slings their version of how to find your purpose so you can win at everything. Of course the only way to really figure it out according to this guru is to purchase their course.

Despite how sore you eyes get as they roll back into your head when gurus talk about purpose, it's a crucial thing to figure out if you want to be happy and fulfilled in your work. Happy people just do better, heck they even earn more, so you want to be happy at work.

> The most competitive people, the ones with the competitive edge, don't look to happiness as some distant reward for their achievements, nor grind through their days on neutral or negative; they are the ones who capitalize on the positive and reap the rewards at every turn. - The Happiness Advantage

Nor is happiness some far flung thing you get once you have success and money and that six pack. The Happiness Advantage shows us that happiness and contentment come before success, not as a result of success.

Being happy at work will also translate into being happy at home. That means being a better parent and spouse because you don't feel so stressed out. You'll have a longer fuse and thus be able to make better decisions.

So, how is it that we find our purpose? I'd love to tell you some magic formula to find your purpose, but I don't have it. No one has it and if they tell you they do, they're lying. You need to run as far away as possible.

What I can do is give you some questions you can ask yourself if you want to find your purpose. Then you've got to start running some tests (we'll come to that) to see which activities are bringing you energy and which ones are not.

I didn't always have filter documents

I started my business as a web developer. I loved the technology. I got to dig in to hard problems and get paid well for it. I was (am) good at building membership sites for people. I made really good money doing it. Seriously, I'd regularly be in the $500 per hour range or more and had lots of people waiting to become clients.

The problem was that when I wasn't working I wasn't getting paid. This meant that I'd feel bad every time I wasn't at the computer writing code for someone. Regular holidays barely happened. I'd always feel like I had to put just a few more hours in.

I'd stress out when I'd have a Saturday with the kids and want to put a bit more time in with clients. At the beginning maybe we needed the extra revenue, but after a year or two in business I was just working extra. The little bit of extra income didn't change our standard of living in any profound way.

I looked up one day and realized that I was sending my kids to the TV instead of hanging out with them. I was trying to get just a bit more work done. I would almost never take a statutory holiday with my family without starting really early and doing a bunch of work first.

I'd always be saying that I needed one more hour to get some work done.

In short, I had built a business that took me away from the things that mattered most. I believe that: If you've built a great business but have a broken marriage and relationships YOU'VE FAILED.

I had said that a number of times to myself. I'd even written about it, but I wasn't living it. I wasn't living it because I wasn't looking at my filtering documents regularly and evaluating my business against what I said I wanted.

Right now we're going to build out our filter documents. You're going to use them to run every idea through. Not just business ideas, but ideas for where you're going to take your family. If your new business idea means that you're walking further away from what you say you want, then you're not going to do it. At the very least you're only going to keep it up if you change it drastically so it matches up with the life you want to live.

If you're married or have a long term partner, get them to do this work as well. Don't do it together, but when you're both done, bring the filter documents together and compare them.

There is a free workbook for all of these activities. You can get it here.
curtismchale.ca/recommends/focus-email

Find Your Purpose Activity 1: Quadrants

The first exercise I have all my coaching clients do is figure out their 4 Quadrants. To do this take a piece of paper and fold it top to bottom then side to side. Now unfold it and you'll have four different boxes. Each of these boxes represent one of the four most important areas of your life.

These are not the things that others tell you should matter. They're not the things that matter to your spouse. They're not what you think someone in your position should care about. These are the four areas that you value the most.

When you look back in 5 years, if you've accomplished what you intend in these four areas will you consider your life successful so far?

You don't have to use these, but here are some suggestions for your Quadrants.

- Family
- Business
- Finances
- Travel
- Health
- Food
- Volunteer
- ...

My quadrants are:

- Family
- Fitness
- Travel
- Business

Put these four things big and bold as headings in each quadrant. Under each quadrant put down some bullet points that cover what you want the area to look like in 5 years. It doesn't matter if they're crazy, dream big.

In my Business Quadrant I have:

- Bring a whole family up for coaching on an outdoor trip with child care provided so I can work with the couple without distractions
- Only need to be online two days a week

I'm not in a position yet to bring my coaching clients up with their spouses and kids and take them on a trip as we do coaching alongside my wife and kids, but that's where I want to get to. I have that in mind with every decision I make as I build my business, and that's the purpose of your filter documents.

I'm also not in the spot yet were I could ignore the internet three days a week if I want. I need to get online and check in with people regularly. I can't put everything down on a random Monday to take my kids on a hike, but I'm working towards it.

It's not uncommon for you to look back at this after you've started and feel the need to revamp it. Most people go back over these things three or four times before they've thought long and hard enough to be happy with their goals.

Find Your Purpose Activity 2: 5 Year Life

Next up is your 5-Year-Life. This is similar to your Quadrants and you should do them both because each exercise brings out different things. It's entirely common for you to revise your Quadrants as you do the essay and to revise the essay as you look back at your Quadrants.

You should be handwriting this essay. No typing, write it down by hand. The thing is that when you're writing by hand you slow down and think about what you're writing more. Every time I've had clients go back and do the work over by hand, they've got so much more out of it and have been happier with the work. It's felt "done" when on paper in a way that the digital version never did.

The goal of this essay is to dream about your life in detail. While the workbook provides a few pages for you to write in, it may not be enough. Grab another sheet of paper and staple it in or do the work in your notebook.

Don't be afraid to go in to detail here. Dig deep. What is the name of the dog you're going to own? How many kids will you have and what are their names going to be?

What colour will you paint your office?

Will you have a climbing wall in your garage, and a weight facility? Will both of these sit under your office which has a deck overlooking your pool? That's part of what is in my essay because it's what I want to work towards.

Here are a few more primer questions to get you started. You can find more in the workbook that goes with this book.

- What would it look like to have good clients?
- What does it mean to me to be a good parent/spouse/partner?
- Where do I want to live?
- What types of vacations do I want to be taking?
- Describe a specific project, what is the client like? How did they find you? What do they do in their business?

- What does your travel look like?
- How much vacation do you take in a year?
- Where do you take your vacations?
- How much time do I want to be working?
- What does your family, health, and work look like?
- What legacy would you like to leave behind?
- What adventures do you want to pursue?
- What accomplishments will you be looking back on?
- Which dreams will you no longer regret pursuing? Why?
- What does your income look like?

Find Your Purpose Activity 3: Antigoals

The final exercise to walk through is to figure out your Antigoals. That means you write down what you never want your day to look like.

My worst day is a bunch of meetings and interruptions to my flow that mean I never get long periods of time to work. I don't want those days. I don't want to be accountable for every minute to anyone, I want to work when it suits me and where it suits me.

I was pretty close to this with my Web Development business. I'd have meetings a few days a week, but only when I made my calendar available to others. I'd regularly have to be in some project management tool updating someone. Despite my best efforts, I'd have others setting my tasks for the day. It would feel stressful to end the day anytime before dinner was on the table, so watching my kids figure skate usually involved more work squeezed in from the stands.

I don't wish that type of crunched life even on the people I don't like.

Once you have a list of the things you never want your day to look like, develop a set of rules for what your day will look like. My rules are:

- I will only take meetings on Friday

- I will be up and working by 6am when my best focus can be used
- I will only check email once a week
- I will plan my next week every Friday and plan my day the night before
- All client projects will be in my project management tool to streamline my process

The first time I did my Antigoals, my web development business got much much better. I limited my call times even more. I said yes to less clients. I got very picky about who I would work with. I always made sure that I was working on high value projects for me and for my clients.

Does every single day 100% conform to these rules for me? Of course not, life happens. The day I wrote this section my wife's parents are visiting so instead of working at 6am and then taking a break in the middle of the day before a few more hours of work, I ran first thing to make sure the car was free for them if they wanted to go somewhere.

The point is that most days and weeks conform to my ideals and every time I get off track, I look back to my Antigoals and change how the next week will run so it's not sending me down the same path I hate.

Get Your Spouse To Do The Work

Like I said at the beginning, if you've got a spouse or a long term partner around, make sure you do all this work at the same time. Not together, but each of you do the Quadrants and the essay and the Antigoals. Then come together and talk about what each of you wants.

One client I had wanted to run a hobby farm. He was so passionate about the farm and was sure that his wife was 100% on board with running a farm. While she did like the idea, she wanted to run a farm after they had done a bunch of travelling. She wanted to travel in the next 5 years and then work towards that farm. He wanted to build the farm now.

With the different ideas down on paper and talked over, they figured out how to navigate the goals together so that they were on the same page. If they hadn't written down what they wanted on their own how much longer would they have continued to be on totally different pages? How much harm would have been done to their relationship before they got on the same page?

Would they have ever got on the same page or would the marriage have ended in divorce?

Once you've talked about where you each want to be, develop these documents for your family and life together. Make rules about what you won't do as a family, like not just let the kids watch TV all the time.

If you're not on the same page, don't be surprised to find that you're frustrating each other with the life decisions you each are making. You both need to be on the same page if you want to stay together.

Don't be surprised if you have to keep coming back to these filter documents over the course of a few months to get on the same page. One client I had took over a year to dig in to what parts of life they each felt was important. It took them months to understand why they each put priority in different areas. It was a while before they got something down that they were both happy with for their lives going forward.

While it was a long hard time, they both say that since they got on the same page, they've never had a better relationship. The work is worth it, if you're willing to do it.

When Do you Do These Filter Documents?

For some of you it's almost the middle of the year. For some, you grabbed this book as the year started. Others will be reading this in November feeling like you just wasted a year. The time you picked up this book doesn't mean you can't start these documents now. I go back over my filtering documents every three months when I start a new journal.

I at least rewrite the work I did previously and check it against where I am at currently. Am I still making steps in the proper direction? Do I have any projects that are off course?

Am I letting something get worked on without requalifying as a valid project? Is that project sticking around just because it has some momentum even though I no longer care about it?

Once a year I start from scratch with the foundation documents. Once I've done them at the start of my year without referencing old work, I'll go back and visit the older versions and see if there is something I missed. Usually there are a few things that were missed. Some of them matter and some of them have changed for me so I don't worry about it.

By checking in at least when I start a new notebook, and as I plan my new year, I am in touch with my filtering documents at least 4 times a year. This is crucial if you want to make sure that your not taking your business way off track.

Now that you've got your personal filter documents in hand, and your family documents for reference it's time to start generating ideas. We need to start by generating ideas so that we have a bunch to test against where we want to be.

The next chapter is all about that idea generation process. Get ready to write a whole bunch more down as you find an idea that can kick your life in to the next level

Take The Filters Challenge

If you're ready to get started, it's time to take the challenge. Do the workbook to build your filter documents. Get your spouse/partner to do it as well. Share a picture of one or both of you with your filter documents on Instagram, Twitter or Mastodon with the hashtag #theartoffocus

I'll be picking one shared picture a month for a free coaching session with me.

2

FINDING YOUR FOCUS

I t's great to have a list of the way you want your life to be, but it's a hard thing to look at when your life is far away from that ideal. Especially since most of us, myself included, look at others and it seems like they have it mostly together.

In this chapter we're going to generate a bunch of ideas that you can use as your focus. These are the ideas that will help you get to that life you've written about in your filtering documents.

Brainstorming Your Single Focus

Now that we have our filtering documents in place, we're ready to start to figure out how we can niche our business. To help ensure that you don't build a business you end up hating the last step of working on your niche will be taking all your ideas and running them through your filtering documents. We do this after generating our ideas so that we can try to make sure that we don't build ourselves some zombie like business that we want to run away from.

In Part III we'll look hard at testing our ideas in the marketplace. We always want to filter our ideas through where we want to go before we test in the marketplace because we don't want to end up with a profitable business that we hate.

The first two questions you need to ask yourself as you look for your niche is, what is your most profitable service and what is the work you enjoy doing the most? Your most profitable service is not likely the one that you charge the most for. In fact when I did this work I found that my most profitable development work was not custom code work. It was fairly straight forward site setup work at a fixed rate for a fixed scope.

For me this "fairly basic" work was also the least stressful work. Doing site setups I almost never hit an issue that would mean a day used up trying to solve a problem for which I didn't even have the right question yet. Not hitting random issues like that is why it's the most profitable work. There is little to no time spent that's not moving the project forward.

I find the work easy. The work is 90% the same from client to client. The problems I'll hit are 99% the same ones that will have well known solutions. With the right process I can do two or three of them in a week and be earning $6 - $9k a week working mostly half days on the projects.

The next question to ask yourself is, what do you stand against in your industry? For web marketing people, I stand against some video series selling you on something without a price up front. I'm against fluffy articles that don't give you actionable advice on what you can do this week to make your business better.

I'm against a bunch of random content upgrades, which is why when people sign up to my list they get access to every single content upgrade I have from any post ever. Once you join, you're in the club. I don't want you to jump through any more hoops at all.

I'm against the internet marketer that wants you to sign in to Facebook Messenger to get a PDF download that then sends you text messages, and Facebook messages, and emails and all from different people who don't realize that they're all talking to the same person. Coming back from vacation with 23 emails, 5 text messages, and 8 Facebook Messages is a terrible thing to do to anyone.

All of these tactics drive me bonkers and make me close said internet marketing site. No matter how excited I was about the product to start with.

For web development work, I'm against the crazy back and forth that can go on with pricing. This is why I state my pricing for setting up a membership site plainly on my site. If you reach out to me, you know the price before you get in touch. If it's too much, then you don't get in touch.

It's also worth asking yourself what type of work you're doing in your free time? At one point I could answer firmly with more coding and exploring how to become a better developer. Now I'd have to say at night I'm reading about running a good business. I'm digging deep into books across many fields so that I can help the people that I coach. I still enjoy much of being a developer, but I'm no longer doing it in my off time. Gone are the days when I can't wait to get back at the computer to write a few more lines of code.

Another crucial set of questions to ask yourself around your niche, is how much money do you need to make every month? I like breaking it up in to two different groupings. First, what is the break even point for your business? Where can you pay all your bills and still live a reasonably comfortable life? To me comfortable means that you can afford the activities your family likes to do and while you can't do everything, you aren't constantly saying "I can't afford that" about everything you want to do.

The second phase is, how much would it take per month right now to feel like you were living in luxury? No I'm not talking about the luxury where you wouldn't worry about crashing a Ferrari, I'm talking about the luxury that would let you take the 2 or 3 vacations you want a year to wherever you wanted travelling in style. The type of luxury that would let you get some extra help with child care so that you can date your spouse a few times a week.

What will People Pay For?

That's where most people stop. They tell you to pursue all the things you love and you're good at, and they rarely talk about what your clients are willing to pay for. This is why so many small businesses die. They're marketing a service they can do easily, but one no customers value. If they do value it, they don't value it much so they want to pay very little for it.

In asking what people will pay for, there are a few questions we need to answer.

First, what problem can you solve with your skills that people feel a pinch on. If you're solving a fairly generic, easy problem then it's not going to be all that valuable. But that doesn't mean you have to go for something complex.

I find setting up a membership site easy, because I've done it hundreds of times. My clients don't find it easy. Many of them have spent a bunch of time trying to make it all work, and they have a list of problems bigger than their arm. Most of the problems they're trying to solve now that they've spent a bit of time on the site, they didn't even know existed when they started.

This is where I come in with my experience. I can answer their questions and set up their site. I can tell them what type of content works for emails so that they can just worry about building out the content they need for their membership site.

The second question to ask is, how expensive is the problem they have? If you're catering to beginners in business, then it may not matter how valuable your work is. If they are starting out and don't have money, they won't be spending it.

A friend of mine helps established developers negotiate salaries with large companies like Apple, Microsoft, Google...and any other number of large companies you've heard of. He's helped them go from $100k a year to $150k plus a whole bunch of stock and other benefits.

He solves an expensive problem.

While I can help you get started in the freelance field if you're just coming out of school, you are most likely much better served by learning the ropes at a traditional job. I target my coaching towards established freelancer's looking to get in to a multiple 6-Figure salary. I target people established in their job that are wanting more control over their time. They want to head out on their own and have the skills they need to do work, they need someone to help them build a transition. Both groups need someone to help them build processes around vetting clients, and time management, and contracts so that they can build the business they're dreaming of.

One client in particular was looking to leave her job. The first contract she signed was over $10k a month. She walked in to the meeting with the company offering her a job and not wanting a consultant. She left with a few hours on site a week and over $10k a month in her pocket.

Positioning her was an expensive problem.

Third, you should be asking yourself how repeatable the problem is. I prefer to stick to problems that have a fairly high repeatability factor. This means that I can build out a process and use it many times with only slight tweaks to fit a client profile. I found that this is the most profitable work I can do.

The other side of that is highly customized service. If you're an expert and have a good range of experience you can charge very well for customized services.

The problem is in the middle. When you don't quite have enough experience to get really high rates because you're not yet the leading expert. The complexity isn't any less, but you can't charge as much.

For most people, the place to start is with a problem that is fairly expensive and has a large amount of repeatability.

The final question is, how do your prospects talk about their problems? We'll cover this in it's own chapter later so hang tight if you don't know how to figure this out.

In short, you should understand how your prospects talk about their problems. Are they using language that is urgent? This would signify that the problem is expensive and thus one to dig deeper in to. If they're using language that trivializes the problem then it may not be one you want to get in to because you won't be able to charge much for your services.

With these questions, you should have a solid set of business ideas you could pursue as your niche. Since you can't pursue them all, it's time to start ranking them.

Ranking the Value of Your Business Ideas

The first question you need to ask as you rank ideas is: "Are there any ideas if successful that will make the rest of this easy or irrelevant?"

These are ideas that if successful will mean the rest of your ideas don't matter. You don't need to bother with them because the single idea working well means you don't need the income from any of the other ideas.

If there are one or two that fall into that category, then put the number 0 beside them. You should at most have 2 or 3 of these. If you come up with 20, then you're lying to yourself. It's unlikely that every idea you have is a winner on this scale.

If you are unsure if an idea will make the rest of your work easier or irrelevant, then it should get a 10. Ideas that you know won't negate the rest of your work get a 20.

The second evaluation to put your ideas though is, how much work will it take to implement them? If you say that a podcast with 1,000,000 listeners is that single idea which will make everything else easy or irrelevant, what work will it take to get to that many subscribers? The fact is, it will be a huge amount of work to get to 1 Million listeners. It's likely a multi-year project to get there. So when you rank that idea it's going to get a big high ranking for difficulty.

You should use a Fibonacci sequence to rank your ideas. That's a sequence of numbers like: 1, 2, 3, 5, 8, 13, 21, 34...The harder an idea is to implement, the higher the number.

We don't use a standard 1, 2, 3, 4, 5, 6...sequence because it can be really hard to distinguish between something that is a 5 or a 6 in difficulty. It's much easier to decide if an idea is a 5 or an 8.

If you're not sure about the idea, then break it down to a number of parts you are sure about. Rank the difficulty of each of these parts and then add up all the parts to get the total difficulty of the project.

The next filter for your ideas is to step back and ask if this is a 10% improvement idea or a 10x idea? Will they increase your revenue by 10x or 10%? Will they mean that instead of working 5 days a week, you can take a day or two totally off every week or a week off a month?

10x ideas are ones that will launch you into the stratosphere. They're blog posts that will add hundreds or thousands of people to your email list. 10% ideas will have a trickle effect. They'll bring in a few new people, but if they're successful they won't change your life or business all that much.

Your 10x ideas should get a 1 beside them and your 10% ideas get a 20.

Now with your scoring done, you should be looking harder at the items with the lowest scores. If you're not sure how it works in practice I'll show you with an example from my current ideas. I'll limit it to three ideas, but there are far more on my list. My first idea is to take a plugin I have written for a client and make it available for sale. This plugin would require you purchase product A before you can purchase product B. It would be something that could be useful alongside the current membership plugin I own but it's fairly niche.

The second idea is doing a series of tutorials for Easy Digital Downloads (EDD). It would be positioned for users of EDD so that developers could get their clients to purchase the tutorials and take some of the training load off of developers.

The third idea is relaunching a book I wrote that was called Don't Be An Idiot: Run a Viable Freelance Business. It's aimed at beginning freelancers that want a plan to move from where they are now into something they control.

Here is how my scores break down.

The membership plugin ranks as a 20 because I don't think that it has the chance to make the rest of my work easier or irrelevant. It's only a 13 to get it going because I have the working code. All I have to do is package it up for sale. It ranks as a 20 because it's a 10% project. I think it will be one among many WordPress plugins some of which have more features around membership sites on top of the single feature mine will have.

The EDD training ranks as a 10. It might make the rest of my work easy or irrelevant, but it might not. It might be just another set of training videos. It gets the highest score of 21 for implementation because it's a lot of work to record videos. I'll have to maintain it and attract a whole bunch of people to it with yet more videos that do training. If it works though, I think that it has a good chance of being a 10x thing so it gets a 1 on that score.

Finally, the relaunch of my old "Idiot" book. I read through it at Christmas and it's really quite good. I'm not sure why I stopped selling it. I do have some edits, but nothing that needs a bunch of research. I just need to go back through it over a few days to get a first draft done. It gets a 0 because it has a high chance of bringing in a bunch of new freelancer's to my marketing stream. It's low score of 5 is because it's mostly there and doesn't need external resources to complete it. It gets a 1 because it is a 10x idea.

Once you've scored your ideas, take them and sit down with someone you trust. Make sure your rankings are removed so you don't bias them. Ask them to help you work through the ideas and give them a rank with the same methods you just used above. Take their rankings and add them with your rankings and then divide by two (or three if you ask two other people) to get the average ranking.

Usually you will have one or two clear winners out of this scoring process. If you have a whole bunch, then go back through the scoring process throwing out all but the top contenders. Get more specific with the implementation ranking by breaking each one down in to the parts they will take to get going.

Once you've done that second pass through with your top ideas, you should be down to the one or two that are the best options.

We're almost, but not quite ready to start picking ideas off the list to start testing your niche in the real world.

Run These ideas through your filter documents

You should have some good contenders for ideas worth pursuing. The problem that many people encounter here is that they head down a path and build a business that sucks.

Oh sure, they have some money, but every aspect of the business makes them trade off things that the never wanted to trade off.

They're missing breakfast with the kids, dates with their spouse. They don't exercise and they eat like crap. All in the name of...money or success. Some external metric for validation that others have convinced them matter as a measurement of success.

Before you start to work on any of the ideas on the list, it's time to take a look back at our filter documents. That's your Quadrants, 5-Year-Life, and Antigoals.

Which of the ideas will lead you to compromise on things you've said you care about? If you said you want to travel and not be online much, which ideas need you to be online.

Don't give me any crap about "Oh in 2 years I'll have staff so I can create that company which will let me do the travelling I wanted to do". You won't have staff and even if you do, they take way more management than you expect. You'll still need to be online more than you wanted.

Just don't build that company at all and move on to another idea.

Throw out all the ideas that mean you need to spend a bunch of time violating the things you care about. None of the rankings matter if you're building a business that's going to increase your stress and make you compromise what matters to you.

Do You Have the Career Capital?

In his great book, So Good They Can't Ignore You, Cal Newport introduces the idea of career capital. This is the thought that to get people to buy in to your ideas you must have built up the capital needed to push your idea forward. You must spend your career capital to get buy in for the ideas you have.

You need to ask yourself this question when you look at all your ideas because it will inform which ones you can go forward with. If you're just beginning as a writer, you don't have the career capital to charge top rates. You don't have a system to produce high quality work for your clients. Why would someone trust you as you work to build your business idea to something of substance.

This may mean that at first you need to spend time building that career capital. As you rank your ideas you need to take that in to account.

How will you build yourself in to an expert in your field?

How will you gain the trust of your prospects to turn them in to clients?

What will it take to get to expert status?

Take a look back at your ranking for the difficulty of implementation, do you need to adjust them to take building career capital in to account? Will it take you a year of building your name before you get to a spot where you can launch your idea well?

If your not sure don't worry. Part III will go over ways to test your idea in the market and ways to bring leads in. These will help you figure out what type of traction you can expect to see as you get started.

When I first started coaching I had no plan to do it. Oh sure I have a Counselling Degree, but the standard counselling method just wasn't for me. I kept getting calls from other freelancer's asking how to navigate a project pricing negotiation process. I was getting asked to review proposals for my competition because they wanted to know what I thought of them.

I was fielding calls from small companies to talk about their client vetting process and every email they sent to prospects.

One call in particular sealed the deal for me to believe that I should pursue coaching. I was having sushi and my friend Brian called. He had just been talking to a client about a long term retainer. He had quoted them $2000 a month for his services, but really felt like he was worth $3000. He had been too scared to ask for it though.

Over 15 minutes while I snacked on my lunch I talked Brian

through why he was worth much more than $3000. Heck I put it at $5-6k a month. We talked about how to reposition himself for their conversation the next day so that he could get paid more.

That 15 minute confidence boosting call meant that Brian got $4000 a month for a 2 year retainer. That's $24k extra a year a 15 minute call added to his bottom line. When I got the text telling me about what he negotiated I sat back and realized that I did have the career capital and expertise to coach.

Without having already negotiated contracts with Fortune 500 companies, and running a healthy 6-Figure freelance business, I wouldn't have been able to help Brian. I would have only been able to commiserate with him in his fear about not going for what he thought he was worth.

Because I had spent years building a solid 6-figure freelance business I had established myself as an authority. I could start to spend some of my career capital as I started building my coaching business.

Now that you've got a bunch of ideas ready to go, we're ready to move on. The next step to build focus in to your life and work is understand what you're willing to do to win.

Are you dreaming of the end only? Do you want to be a recognized author or are you up for writing 1000 words day in day out in obscurity for a while? The end you want only comes because you put the work in.

Do the Idea Generation Challenge

Once you've got your ideas written down and ranked, take the challenge. Take a screenshot and tag it with #theartoffocus on Twitter, Instagram or Mastodon.

I'll be picking one shared picture a month for a free coaching session with me.

3

PLANNING YOUR IDEAS

N ow that you've got a big list of ideas, it's time to take it another step further because having some ideas without a plan is a terrible idea. In this chapter we're going to make sure that you have a plan put together so that your ideas have the highest chance of succeeding.

What Would It Look Like?

There was a time when I first started my business that I wanted to charge $10k or more for my work. I longed to do it, but I wasn't ready yet. I dreamed of being valuable enough to a company to charge $3000 a week for my services, but I was nowhere near providing that type of value to my customers.

I stumbled around for a few years before I started asking the right question. What level of service would I need to provide to have that much value to my clients?

That question meant I started sending Monday updates for the week and then provided a wrap up email on Friday. I started doing weekly phone calls with my clients to make sure that we were on the same page.

Once I had these things in place, I landed my first 5-figure project. Then my second, and my third was over $30k all in the course of a few months.

I easily sold myself at $4000 a week to Fortune 500 companies, and I didn't work Friday's for them. They knew that was business development time. These same companies were happy to wait weeks for me to be available, because I was the expert they needed.

As you look at your few business ideas that should take the least amount of time to execute and have the biggest impact, it's time to get serious about them. No more guessing which one will take the least amount of time. Do some serious thinking.

To do this we start with the single question that turned my business in to what I wanted it to be: "What would it look like to _____?"

If you want to launch a YouTube channel that does reviews then the question is: "What would it look like to launch a review YouTube channel that brings in $XXXX per month?"

Then you can start figuring out what it's going to take. If you're looking at that YouTube channel then the first thing you need to realize is that you can't monetize your YouTube channel until you have 4000 hours watched in the last 12 months and 1000 subscribers. That means your first question is really: "What would it take to have a YouTube channel than meets the threshold for monetization?"

You'd need to figure out approximately how many videos you'll need. What quality will your videos need to be? What products are the most popular in the industry that you're targeting? How will you need to share your videos to get enough traction with them so that YouTube starts to show them in their recommended videos?

What other ways can you monetize your video content? Could you use Amazon links or other affiliate links to the products you're reviewing?

How many subscribers/viewers do you probably need to get to your income number? Is it 1000 or 10,000 or 100,000?

No, you won't be able to know exactly how many viewers you need, but you'll know the order of magnitude. There is a large difference between 10,000 and 100,000 so which one is it?

Do this thinking for the few ideas that have come so far. When I run my ideas through this stage in the process I give it an entire afternoon to work on 2 or 3 ideas. Usually it's an hour or so of work, then a walk while I think about the ideas more and then another hour or two of work.

Even then, I will come back to the ideas a number of times over the next week or two before I feel like I've delved deep enough to understand them. The first few hours usually just establish all the questions I need answered before I'm ready to map out all the work that is needed.

Roadblocks

Next up is determining your roadblocks. What will stop the idea from happening? Unfortunately so many people look at the word roadblock and figure it's a bad word. Far from being a bad word, roadblocks are a great constraint on our ideas.

If you figured that it would take 1000 subscribers and 1000 videos to get the income you want, but you you realize that the most you can do is 1 video a week to match your market then you're an 19 year journey to get to where you want to be. That is a roadblock, but what if you flip the script.

What if you did review videos that were 10x better than the competition in your niche? Could you then monetize a much smaller number of subscribers, or get more views and thus hit the income you want with a much smaller number of videos?

I go on a walk with my friend Ron every few weeks. Recently we were talking about another friend of his that wants to publish a children's book. After about an hour of discussion on people to get in touch with and tactics to use when you publish a book we started talking about the most important question.

What work is his friend willing to do?

Are they willing to go to every library in the area in person and ask about doing a reading of their children's book?

Are they willing to reach out to every homeschool group in the area to do a book reading?

Are they willing to produce a set of colouring pages to go with the book to start to collect emails which they can leverage as they do the follow up books they have planned?

Will they email 100 podcasts a week to get on 3?

Are they just dreaming of the end, having a published children's book?

In this case, he wasn't sure, but that's the question you need to ask yourself now that you have a better idea of what it's going to take to launch your idea.

Are you going to do the work?

You can't blame someone or something outside. You have to take ownership of the success or failure of your idea.

Is your spouse willing to sacrifice so that the idea can win?

As I finished up this book and looked at launching it I had a crazy six week schedule on the books. I had to record and edit audio. Before I could start that I had to edit the book, and build a launch list, and finalize the title and cover. I had to set up CreateSpace and learn a whole new launch sequence because I had paid for Self-Publishing School and I wanted to launch this book to success that my other books hadn't seen.

That meant I had to do some weekend work to make it all happen. Cynthia (my wife) had to buy in for that. We had to set bounds on what that would mean and how we would do it as a family.

In our case it meant getting dropped off at the library a few times with my iPad in hand so I could edit audio. I'd edit for an hour or two then walk down to the river where my family was playing in the water. I could stash my bag in the car and then join them for some time in the local swimming hole.

Once the book is launched we'll evaluate the time commitment again and adjust so that we feel balanced going in to the school year.

If you're not going to do the hustle that it's going to take to get your idea off the ground I only see two choices for you.

First, stop because you clearly aren't confident in the idea to make the sacrifices you need to make it happen. It's time to figure out why. Did you not choose an idea that you believed in. Did you not do the work to vet your idea? Is it not scored correctly?

If you have realized that the idea isn't high enough value, then go back and pick another one. While some people will find the right idea the first time, some will go back and forth through ideas a number of times before they find one that they can make work.

The second option requires a bit more personal honesty. Are you just scared? Do you want to have the outcome without the work in the middle?

While I look forward to my mountain running races, the thing I love the most is the training. Even on some of the local trails that I barely consider trails because they weave through subdivisions, I love the act of training.

Yes I have a goal for the race, but the process is just as appealing as the goal. Do you look forward to the process of building your idea? You have to if you want it to succeed.

Dreaming one day of being an author but never writing will mean it won't happen. Sure the idea of writing in some quiet space is appealing to many, but who wants to write 1000 words a day in relative obscurity for years first? Very few people. Only those of us that enjoy the process of writing.

Planning

We've already talked a bit about planning as it pertains to your spouse, but you need to take a step back and see what's going on in your life. I'm working to launch this book in July and August. That's the summer and for many people this is a time when they have a bunch of extra random commitments.

They're on vacation and friends are visiting. They're heading to the beach or river regularly. Shorter days are normal in the midst of the summer for most people.

There is always something though. After the summer there is Thanksgiving and the Christmas. Around here the winter brings skiing and snowshoeing. After Christmas, it's a short hop to spring break and then you're almost back to summer with it's long weekends and time spent on the water.

Around my house we have 5 birthdays as well, plus my brother and sister in law who live in the same town. That spreads them out fairly evenly as one per quarter. For almost every birthday my in-laws come out for 10 days. That means every quarter I have at least one 10-day period where I'm not quite as productive. I don't take the whole time off, but family is around the house with the kids so I end up taking longer lunches and more coffee breaks in the midst of the day.

This is the final filtering step you're going to do as we figure out which ideas you're going to move on. You need to step back and look at the big picture of your coming months and see how your work is going to fit in to what you have going on.

Like I said, this 6-week block is busy around my house as I finish off book edits and launch the book to what I hope will be amazing fanfare. Given your schedule, can you launch your idea as fast as you hoped?

If you were going to do review videos, do you know how long one is going to take you? What block of time each week can you put aside? How many videos do you have to finish in a week?

My favourite big picture planning tool is the 6ft by 3ft Neu Year Calendar. I use it for all the vacations, and visits and birthdays. At a glance I can see what my big picture is. I can tell when I have more time to push hard and when I'll be annoyed with life if I'm trying to get lots of work done because I won't have the time I want.

You have an idea of what it would take to launch your idea, do you have that time in the next three months? What will you need to rearrange to have the time? If not in the next three months, then when are you going to do it?

Is one of the other ideas smaller, but still possible with what you have on your plate currently? Will that smaller idea purchase enough of your time that you could start to move on your big idea?

It's important not to get into the weeds of your week yet, we'll cover building out your week in Part II of the book. We're looking at the big picture so that we can understand what we can and can't do with the commitments we have currently.

You should now have a plan to make sure that you understand how much work it's going to take to get your idea off the ground. You should have run your idea through your filtering documents. You should have some research done in to what your customers want and need, what they're willing to pay for.

That means it's time to move on to Part II of the book. Part II is all about getting control of your time so that you can start to take the steps you need to launch your single focused idea.

If you've struggled with your time management. If you've ever felt like there are more tasks than the week has room for, then Part II is for you.

PART II

PART II: FINDING YOUR TIME

4

YOUR TIME MANAGEMENT SUCKS, LET'S FIX IT

W e spent Part I of this book building the picture of ideal life that we want. Then we took that ideal life and started to generate some ideas that can help us get to it. We made sure that we ran our ideas through our filter documents so that we don't end up building a life that we hate.

Finally, we walked through some planning questions to help us make sure that we anticipated the amount of work that it will take to make our ideas happen. We looked at our big picture schedule so that we were realistic with what we could accomplish.

Now we're going to get more detailed with our planning. What will our days look like? Do you know when it's best to do creative work? Forget all this night owl or early bird crap. For all of us the best time to do creative work is in the morning, whenever that morning is based on your natural schedule.

In his recent book When, Daniel Pink, showed us that we all follow pretty much the same cycle for focus. We have more focus when we wake up in the morning. Our focus wanes throughout the day until it is at its lowest in the afternoon. Then we slowly increase again until we have second peak, though not as high, in the evening.

For morning people, that's an early morning peak say 9-10am. For night owl's, that's a mid-morning peak, say 10-11am. When it's morning for you is irrelevant, mornings are better for your focused work.

With that in mind, this section is going to look at how rest is the precursor to focus. How you can block your time so that you have a plan for the day. How to build a system around you that helps you avoid distractions.

Finally, we'll dig in for those of you that are not self-employed. How do you bring focus to the workplace so that your boss sees the benefits? By bringing focus to your work, you can build the career capital needed to take more control over your time. With more control over your time you will be able to start moving forward faster with the things you want to focus on.

5

THE FIRST STEP IS RESTING PROPERLY

I f you want to be effective with your time, then the first stop is to make sure that you're getting effective rest. Without effective rest, you will never have the energy needed to sustain your work. You'll be running on empty. You'll be unable to give your best ideas all the focus they need.

Don't Bother If You're not getting Proper Rest

There was in interesting study on programmers that looked at the amount of sleep they got against their productivity. It showed that well rested programmers started with a high amount of productivity which then waned as the day went on. If they took a break in the late morning or early afternoon and came back at it, they had another burst of productivity.

Programmers that didn't get adequate rest started with low productivity and just went down all day.

Note that these very productive programmers followed the same rhythms that Daniel Pink found in his book When. That should only reinforce that it's not just programmers that follow this rhythm, it's all of us.

Your body is a machine that needs to be kept tuned properly if it is to run properly. Without proper rest and exercise, you're not going to reach your full potential. We're going to address what that looks like here.

What Proper Rest Looks Like

How many of you try to fool yourselves into thinking that you can run on only 5 hours sleep a night? Yup I said fool yourself, because research says that you can't function well on 5 hours sleep.

According to the National Sleep Foundation, the average adult needs 7-9 hours of sleep a night. That's adults from 18 - 64, it's only after 64 that they change the recommendation to 7-8 hours a night. In fact no category is suggested to get less than 7 hours a night.

Yeah I know you're telling yourself that you're not the average. You're the exception. You're lying to yourself. Everyone wants to be some special snowflake that is the exception, and almost no one is.

You need 7-9 hours of sleep every night if you want to be maximally productive. If you're not getting that much sleep, then it doesn't matter how well you preform, you're operating at less than your maximum capacity.

To win with your ideas in the shortest amount of time possible, you need to be giving them your full focus.

The second question most people want to understand now is, are they larks or night owls or third birds?

You've probably heard of night owls and larks before. Larks love the morning. They get up early and peak in the early morning. They fall off in the afternoon and are done in the evening.

Night owls, are more likely to be found working at midnight than midday. They don't love mornings and peak later in the day.

A third bird is a term coined by Till Ronnenberg and describes about 60% of the population. They are neither complete larks nor complete night owls. You're somewhere in the middle.

The next factor to consider is your age. In general, we're larks as we are kids. Ask pretty much any parent and they'll confirm this as their kids show up in their room at 5:45am ready to go. As we move to our teens we become night owls, which seems to peak around the age of 20. From there we drift back towards being a lark. Most of us over the age of 60 are firmly larks again.

The fastest way to get a good idea of where you are is to figure out your midpoint of sleep when you can choose when to get up. If the midpoint of your sleep is between 12am - 3am then you're a lark. If your midpoint is between 3:30am and 5:30am then you're a third bird and if it's after 6am, you're a night owl.

Once you know this, start planning when you go to sleep every day for what your natural rhythm should be. If you can't do that because of work, we'll talk about strategies to deal with that later.

My wife and I both are firmly larks. My midpoint of sleep is 12:30am. For a number of months we've been sleeping until 7am on Sunday when our kids wake us up. We kept finding that despite getting a bunch of "extra" sleep we felt worse on Sunday than the rest of the week. That's because, you need to stick with your routine for sleep. By breaking out of our routine of 9:30 to bed and 4:30 up, our bodies were thrown off and dealt with it badly.

By simply getting up around 5:30 am instead, and getting an extra hour of sleep, we've both found that our bodies feel more rested and we get that extra hour of sleep. This is close enough to our routine that it doesn't throw it off.

Kids and Sleep

One of the biggest issues we have when it comes to getting to sleep at the right time is that we have kids and by the time we get them to bed we have around 40 minutes to sit before we need to start getting ready for bed as well.

Many nights of the week those 40 minutes are taken up with household chores. We're doing dishes, changing laundry, sweeping the floor because it seems like we eat with animals that jam their face onto the plates and toss food everywhere. That leaves us with little time to connect and we often just want to sit for a bit and spend time together without kids.

One of the things we instituted as soon as our first child was old enough to have a regular bedtime was that after 7pm it's adult time in the house and that kids have to be in bed. They don't have to be asleep, but they need to be quietly in their bed.

Our oldest (7) will read. Our middle child (4) will play with stuffed toys or hide in her fort and tell herself stories. Our youngest (2) will talk with her older sister and join in on some of the stories from her crib. Sticking with this idea of kids in bedtime has been great when our kids tell us they're not sleepy, I'm not telling them to go to sleep I'm telling them to stay in their bed.

Most times all but our oldest will be asleep shortly after getting in bed. This has left us time to hang out, but planning well for this every night has meant that we start taking steps earlier in the day to make it happen.

Most times that means that as dinner is getting finished one of the parents, and sometimes one of the kids, is starting the dishes. It means that usually one parent is doing baths for our youngest two kids while the other is doing dishes and changing laundry.

We'd both rather sit during dinner, or have help during bath time, but if we do that then we end up doing the chores later instead of having them out of the way so we can talk with each other. This also means that the nights where one parent is home and the other is working till bedtime, which happens 4 nights a week here, that single parent does the dishes and handles all the chores so that after the kids are in bed we still have clear time to spend together.

Another trick we do is to have a dinner date after the kids are in bed. We'll order from one of our favourite restaurants and eat after our kids are in bed.

We used to make excuses and stay up late, paying for it the next day by feeling exhausted, but by getting intentional about our time before the kids are in bed we have got more time together. Last night, we had close to two hours to talk and connect with no chores hanging over our heads.

You have to stop making excuses for not getting enough sleep if you want to win with your work. You have to prioritize good rest, or you're short changing yourself.

Going to Sleep The Right Way

Now that we have the opportunity to get to sleep at the right time for us, what does it take to get to sleep well? I admit that I've rarely had issues falling asleep. It often drives my wife nuts as I head to bed and she comes up a few minutes later to me being passed out. I'll ask in the morning when she came to bed and the answer is 15 minutes after me, but I have no memory of it.

As I've worked with my coaching clients, one of the best systems I've found to help them get to sleep on time is the 10, 3, 2, 1, 0 Sleep Formula.

Here is how it goes in short:

- 10 hours before bed - No caffeine
- 3 hours before bed - no food or alcohol
- 2 hours before bed - no more work
- 1 hour before bed - no more screen time (that means TV, phones and computers)
- 0 is the number of times you hit the snooze button

There are a few parts that are most problematic for people. First is the 10 hour caffeine restriction. People just love their coffee or soda. The problem is that caffeine acts as a blocker for this fancy chemical called adenosine. Adenosine binds to receptors in your brain and when enough of them have found the proper receptors you feel tired.

Caffeine acts like a key that fits the same lock, but doesn't turn it. So it's blocking the adenosine from binding to the receptor sites in your brain. It's not replacing your need for sleep, it's just covering up the issue.

It's a classic way of putting lipstick on a pig. It's still a pig, just one in lipstick. You're still tired, you're only masking the symptoms of the problem and buying time.

There is a great Ted presentation on the effects of caffeine in our bodies. You can watch it here: https://curtismchale.ca/recommends/ted-sleep

If you want to sleep well, cut the caffeine.

Yes alcohol can make your feel drowsy so it could be easy to believe that it's good for your sleep. You'd be wrong though. The thing about alcohol is that while it makes you feel drowsy, it inhibits better sleep later in the night.

It harms you sleep by turning on Alpha activity during sleep. Alpha activity doesn't happen during normal sleep, and it's happening over top of your regular delta activity which is the deep sleep you need for memory formation.

Alcohol also affects that fancy chemical adenosine by producing a bunch of it fast. This is why you feel drowsy. The problem is that it also leaves fast, so you often wake up in the middle of the night. It's like a sugar high and then you crash once that fast energy is out of your body.

Alcohol also appears to harm REM sleep by reducing the amount of it you get. REM sleep is associated with dreams and when you have an interrupted sleep cycle, REM is usually the part that gets dropped. So on top of any chemical interference that alcohol may run, the extra bathroom trips mean you're getting less REM sleep.

My wife is on the leadership team for our church which starts its meetings around 7pm. They usually stretch until 10:30 or 11 at night and she comes home with a head full of thoughts. She used to try and go right to bed because it was well past her normal bedtime, but always found that her brain was too busy and she couldn't fall asleep.

To combat this, she's taken to journaling when she comes home until she's out of stuff to say.

We get stuck in the same mindset when we don't stop any type of work long before we want to be heading to bed. We have heads full of thoughts and ideas for our work. We are full of things to do and just can't shut down our meat computer.

To combat this, shut down any type of work at least two hours before bed. Keep a notebook around and write down any ideas you have in the last two hours of your day, but don't act on any of them. Nothing will burn down if you wait until tomorrow.

Next up, let's deal with your screen time close to bed. Studies show that the blue light which comes out of our computers, TVs, tablets and phones delays sleep onset and reduced the amount of quality sleep that we get.

More than that I find the worst part of screen time before bed is that we easily lose track of what time it is. For me the bane of sleep is Instagram. I end up looking through the discovery feed and just keep flipping around looking at pictures. None of which I really care about, but they are eye candy that keeps pulling me in.

Your particular sleep poison may not be Instagram, but there is likely something that not only contributes blue light to your night, but also causes you to head to bed later than you wanted to. Maybe that Netflix feature where it just starts the next episode of the show you're watching is your sleep killer.

Either way, shut off that screen an hour before you head to bed. First it's going to help stop you from staying up to late because you lose track of time. Second, it's going to cut the blue light out of your night so that you can get to sleep faster.

There are a few arguments against hitting the snooze button, though there is little real research on it's affects. First, most scientists that study sleep say that you're just better off getting proper rest in that time where you usually hit the snooze button anyway so don't set the alarm early and plan to hit snooze a few times.

Second, if you're overtired already then you're more likely to restart your sleep cycle. That means your body will be dumping chemicals that are all about getting deep sleep. You'll be fighting sleep inertia as you get up from "deep" sleep. There is even the assertion that by hitting snooze, we're training our brains that the alarm sound doesn't really mean it's time to get up.

If you're constantly hitting snooze, the best place to stop that is by getting to bed at the right time so that when your alarm goes off you're ready to get up.

How Naps Clean Your Brain

If you've got kids you've likely fought the battle around getting a 2 year old to take a nap. They insist that it's not needed and you try and cajole them into sleep. All the while you're thinking that you'd kill for a nap and they just don't know how awesome a nap is.

The tired parent is right, naps are amazing for us. All of us would benefit from a short nap daily.

> Sleep scientists have found that even a short nap can be effective in recharging your mental batteries. Naps can even provide an opportunity to have new ideas. Their work shows that you can learn to time your nap to increase the creative boost that it provides, make it more physically restorative, or probe the traffic between the conscious mind and unconscious. Napping in other words, turns out to be a skill. - Rest

Daniel Pink talks about naps being a zamboni for our brain. The same way a zamboni cleans an ice rink, a nap smooths the rough spots of our brains so that we can think clearly.

> Done right, naps can be a shrewd response to the trough and a valuable break. Naps, research shows, confer two key benefits: They improve cognitive performance and they boost mental and physical health. - When

The type of nap that Pink is talking about isn't some hour long, or multi-hour, snooze fest. He recommends what is often called a caffeine nap. This is when you have a cup of coffee and then take a 20 minute nap. The caffeine is hitting your system right around the time your alarm goes off to get you up. It's a double whammy of wake up juice for your brain.

To maximize the benefits that can be had from a nap you should make sure that you have a good nap routine. This will help create a cue for your body that it's time to rest for a bit.

First, before you nap make sure that you have decided what you're going to be doing once you get up. Don't waste the time your brain is ready to fire on all cylinders by using it to decide what on earth you'll be doing. Have a task ready to go.

Second, make sure you have some reasonable comfortable spot to nap in. In one office I had I'd keep my rock climbing crash pad at the office. It was between my house and the climbing area anyway, and it was reasonably soft and almost my height. I could lay it down on my office floor and take a nap.

Now that I'm back at my house, I use my bed to take a nap. If you don't have either of those options, then try to find the most comfortable spot you can and use that for your napping.

Third, try to make the space as dark as possible. I'll use a sleep mask to block out as much light as possible.

Finally, the noise in your environment can harm your naps and your sleep for that matter. I sleep with a white noise machine in the winter and either a fan or an air conditioner running in the summer. While there is research showing that maybe pink noise is better than white noise, I haven't tried it. Really what you're looking for is a sound that masks the other goings on in your office space.

If you like nature sounds, then use that. Passing highway traffic, totally fine. Waves lapping up the shore or rain, go for it. Find something that helps damp down all the other noise that can bring you out of a decent nap.

Then, don't hit snooze. Get up and start on your next tasks.

Getting Rest throughout the day

Naps are not the only type of rest that you can get during the day. We also can use some time away from our screen and office to let our brain recharge. This is why I work three hard hours early in the morning then go for a run or do something else for three hours. I've called it The Mullet Method because I spend the morning focused and let distractions in a bit in the afternoon.

To have an effective active rest you need three things:

1. No screen
2. Some effort
3. Something green

No Screen

> The most creative and most productive workers are the ones who are able to unplug from the office, recover their mental and physical energy, and return to their work recharged - Rest

Yes, space starts with no screen time. If you're just going to flip through Instagram, or Twitter or dive into Facebook, you're fooling yourself. You're not resting. Your brain is being highly stimulated.

Also, you're likely to spend way more time doing these things than you expect. The entire incentive of social media is to keep you there longer and longer. They want your attention.

Dipping into email is the same thing. It's a black hole that will steal any chance you have of focusing later in the day. Email is also where everyone else is telling you what they think is important for you to care about. If you've planned your tasks for after your break, then email is only going to pull your focus away from those things that you planned on doing.

Get away from your screen if you want to rest.

Some Effort

The second thing that you need if you're going to rest is some effort. We too often confuse the word rest, with something non-physical but that is not what I'm talking about. I'm talking about resting your brain so that it's ready to tackle the latter part of your day.

I mean, go for a walk or a bike ride. With my Mullet Method, I usually run between my morning work session and my afternoon work session. That's 1 - 3 hours of hard work up a mountain near our house or around the farm lands we have near us. It gets my blood pumping and means I clear my brain up so that it's ready to focus on tasks later.

If you're not a runner or don't like hard physical exercise, then take a walk. Just make it brisk, you should be breathing just a bit harder than normal. Your heart rate should be up.

Don't tell me you don't have time for that or that it's not the best thing you could be doing. Here's a list of accomplished people that took long walks to think.

- Nikola Tesla
- Ernest Hemingway
- Charles Darwin
- Charles Dickens

Use this space in your day to rest your brain. Think about the projects you're working on and good ideas will come. You'll have new solutions bubble up that you would have missed sitting there staring at your computer screen.

If you can get away from carrying your phone at all then you should do it. Take a pocket notebook with you to write down any ideas you have while you're out. Most of us have been trained by our phones to dive in at the merest hint of boredom.

Boredom is where so many good ideas lay as we let our brain drift along different lines of thought without direction.

Something Green

If you want to maximize the restorative benefits of that effort, then look for something green.

In a 2013 study, researchers found that people are "substantially happier outdoors in all green or natural habitat types than in urban environments." They even took into account who you were hanging out with and what you were doing.

Hanging out with your best friend in the middle of a pack of buildings will not make you happier than being alone in a natural environment like a green space

> When she examined the data, she found that she could tell from their brain waves when people were walking through parks and green space and when they were in busy commercial areas: their minds became calmer and less aroused when they turned from the high street into a park. They didn't zone out completely, though. Natural scenes engage some of your attention without requiring much conscious effort: they provide just enough diversion to occupy the conscious mind, leaving the subconscious free to do its own thing – Rest

Most of us have some small park around us that we can get to. Head to wherever you can find the most green and spend some time walking around there. Let it calm your brain down so that you're ready to dig deep with the rest of your work day.

I started this by saying that without proper rest, trying to have a productive day is a losing battle. You shortchange your ability to do work of value without proper rest the night before, and a proper plan throughout the day to ensure that you can perform well.

Proper rest starts the night before with good sleep practices. It continues throughout the day as we make sure that we are working on the work that is best suited to the rhythms of our day. We help keep ourselves in tip top shape by taking proper breaks during the day.

If you can do these things, you're setting yourself up to have a day where you can produce your best work.

You should have a good idea of how you can shape your day to make rest a priority. A plan to get out in something green so that you can maximize your productivity. This means that you have the best chance of giving your all to your work during your work hours.

Next we're going to dig deep in to planning a week so that you can get the maximum effectiveness out of it. We're going to put rest and family first, because winning at work and breaking relationship is failure. I'm going to show you exactly how I plan my week in my notebook. This is the same system that I use with my coaching students so that they can build a life worth living.

6

TIME BLOCKING

My work today looks like this. I get up have a decent breakfast and then head to my office and start working at or before 6am. I walk in and do the work I had planned without dipping in to any distractions. I just work for a few hours.

Then I take a break for 2 - 3 hours followed by another work session from noon until 3pm. When I'm working I focus and when I'm not working, I barely think about it.

By the end of this chapter you'll see exactly how I do that so that you can be intentional with your day.

The alternative is what most people have and where I started. Most of us have no intention with our day. I certainly wasn't intentional when I started working for myself. I'd get up and eat some breakfast and then decide what I felt like working on.

I'd probably check email first or hop on Twitter. Maybe check out Facebook, and once Instagram came along, totally flip through the discovery stream which is a black hole for me. All of these things were much easier to start with than diving in to some client problem or other high value hard work.

At some point I'd do some work, but often I'd have a nagging feeling in the back of my head that I was already tired, despite doing nothing of worth. I'd have a hard time bringing any focus to my day. It would be a constant fight to stay focused on client work or writing work.

Many times I'd look up part way through the afternoon and realize how late it was. I still hadn't had lunch, but worse I hadn't done anything I needed to do that day. I had produced almost no value.

Slowly over the years I developed what I now call my Mullet Method. I get up early and work from around 6am - 9am. Then I take a two to three hour break where I'll run, or hang out with my kids or run some errands or help out with homeschool activities. Even if I'm doing other things, I take some time to do something with my kids.

Then from around 12pm - 3pm I go back to work.

I call it the Mullet Method, because during my early work block I focus. There are no distractions at all. I put on some music and have no notifications. No one can call me. No Slack notifications. No social media. I read for an hour then I write for two.

It's the afternoon where I may dip in to Slack or check with Twitter to see what's happening. The afternoon is when I check email and deal with the random things that life may throw at me.

I came to this because I found that writing first thing in the morning meant that I could almost always write 1000 - 2000 words in those two hours. I just felt more creative. I had no research to back that up, but I do now.

> First our cognitive abilities do not remain static over the course of a day. During the sixteen or so hours we're awake, they change — often in a regular, foreseeable manner. We are smarter, faster, dimmer, slower, more creative, and less creative in some parts of the day than others. - When

In general, we have more energy first thing in the morning. Even if you're a night owl, you have more energy when you wake up. During this morning peak, we find creativity and focus easier. We stay on task better and produce work that we judge as "better".

Then after 3 - 4 hours we tire out and focus is hard. Creativity takes more effort. We get distracted and pulling ourselves back to the tasks we need to do is hard.

We slowly creep back to a second peak later in the day, in to the early evening.

Now you may say that this isn't you, but the research says that it is. We all follow this path of high focus and easier creativity early in our day with a lull and then a second peak. Despite what everyone says, it's unlikely that you're the exception.

That leads us to the question, how do we plan our day? Are you doing the best work at the right times?

Things You Shouldn't Do In The Morning

I'm sure that most of you have heard about the things you shouldn't be doing first thing in the morning.

Don't check email first thing.

Stay away from social media.

Do your most important tasks first.

Decide those important tasks the night before so that you don't waste your strong creative brain on little decisions like deciding what is most important in the morning.

Heck, choose your clothes the night before so that you don't kill your best brain power on choosing a shirt.

None of this is new, so that means the question is, how do you do it? I can't tell you exactly what will work for you, but I can show you what works for me and what has worked for many of my coaching students. It starts by planning my whole week before the week happens.

Plan Your Week

You'll notice that I use a paper notebook. Despite all the goodness that can come out of digital tools, most times they just let us stick with bad habits. A digital task manager lets us easily move a task into next week, when we still won't have more time. A digital tool easily lets us track 20,000 things, 99% of which we'll never do but just can't bear the thought of saying no to.

I won't go on further here about this because I've written an entire book on Analogue Productivity that details why I think going analogue is a better choice for you. I think that starting with something like I do below, on paper, is the most useful way to start planning your time. Even if you move it to a digital calendar later, starting with paper will help you.

Regardless of the tools you use to plan your week, the method I use can work for you, and has worked for my coaching clients.

Start by blocking out your regular work hours. Notice mine goes from 6am to 6pm. I often start a bit earlier and I almost never work until 6pm, but this still shows the main work hours I could have available to me.

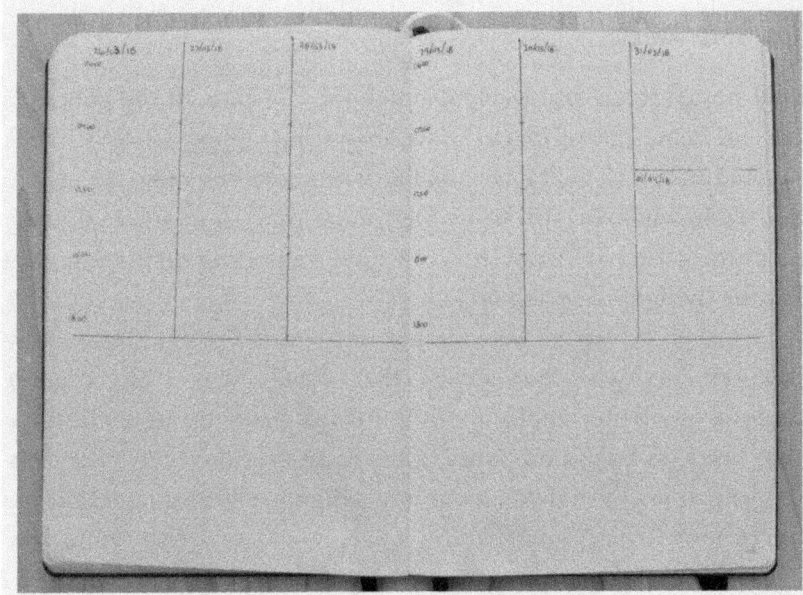

Next, add in any appointments or other family responsibilities you have. Notice in the calendar I'm showing you that I had to be around for skating Tuesday, Wednesday and Thursday. That's not exactly what we're doing now, but my wife is either coaching skating or I'm taking a kid to skating a few nights a week and they're on the calendar because I can't work while skating happens. When my wife is coaching, I'm watching our other two kids.

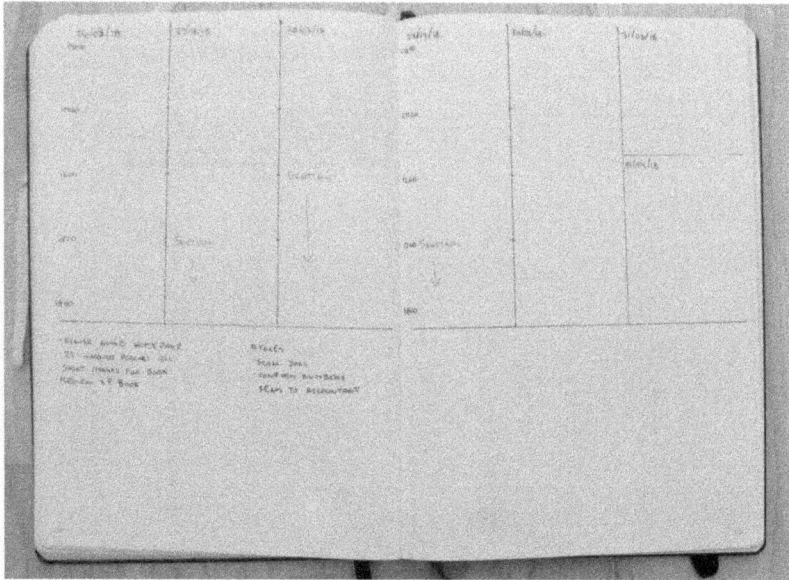

You'll also notice that I have my tasks for the week under my calendar. Those are the big tasks that should have done by the end of the week.

Now add in any self-care that you do. I add in my runs for the week. If you're not doing self-care then you're shortchanging yourself. Seriously, you just read a whole chapter on this. Do your self-care.

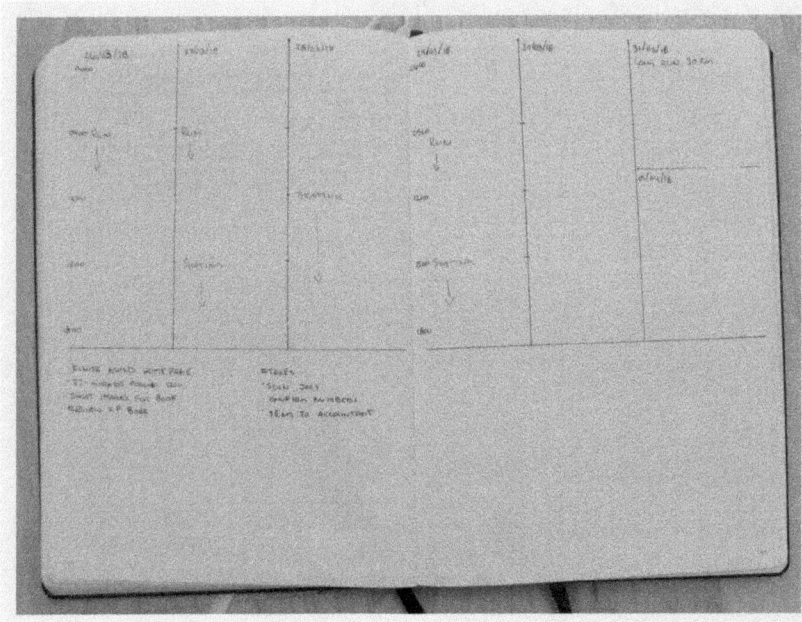

Next up is any client appointments you have in the week. Yes they're work, but they also take time out of when you can do solid focused work to move things forward in your business. You can't be moving client projects forward when you are having meetings with them.

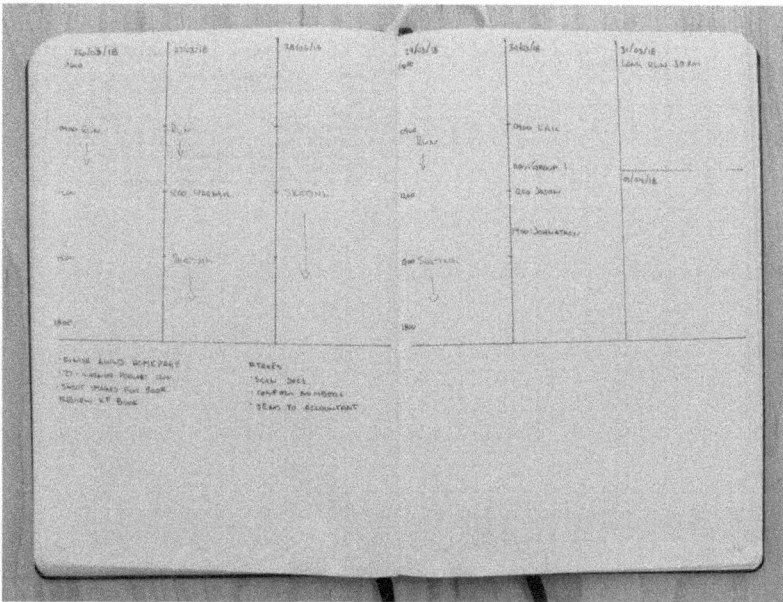

Now I'm ready to put in my work blocks for the week. If I tried to do it before now I'd be surprised, and not in a good way. By adding all the other things to my calendar first, I can see exactly what time is available for client work in a week.

If you don't put all your other commitments on your calendar first, you're no going to get to many of them. You'll miss your self care. You'll figure on a bunch of tasks on a meeting day, only to be surprised when they don't happen.

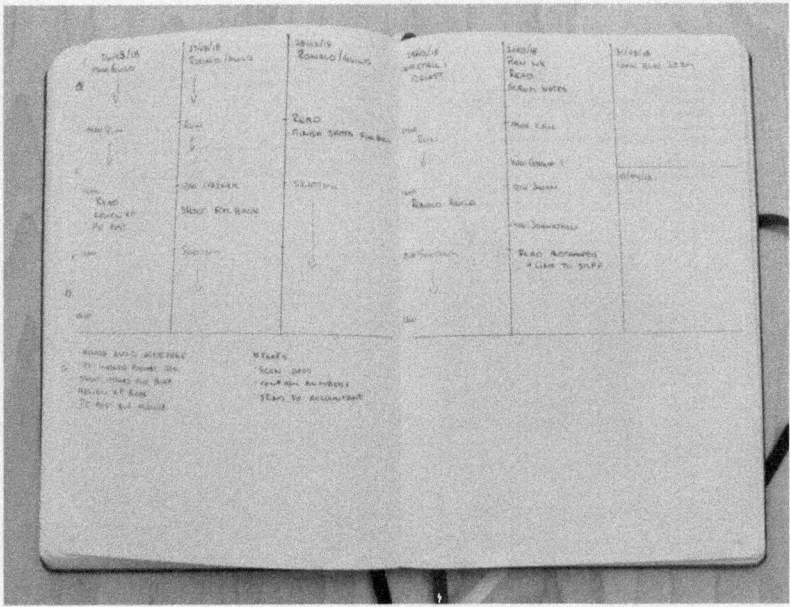

Note that during my work blocks I don't detail the tasks I'm doing. I simply decide what type of work I'll be doing or the client I'll be working for.

Also note that I try to stick to three hour blocks of focused work on one set of problems. Three hours is what I can do now and it's the best focus time I have. I get so much done by knowing that I'm going to spend the next few hours working on a set of problems related to a single project.

Getting to three hours took training though. At first it was hard to spend 25 minutes focused on a single task. Don't bite off more than you can chew. Block out three hours and then maybe break it up into 25 minute segments. Focus for 25 minutes then take a 5 minute break. Aim for as many focused 25 minute cycles as you can inside the time you've set aside for a project.

Your goal should be doing just a bit better at focus every week, not matching up to some ideal you read about. It took me years to train my focus and some days I still don't do well.

To do all this planning I set aside 2 hours on Friday afternoon. It almost never takes me more than 25 minutes, but when I started it did take a lot longer. I set aside 2 hours so that I end my week with a rest as well. No meetings, just 25 minutes of planning then I do what I want, which is often read, but sometimes a walking meeting with a good friend. Sometimes just sitting down in the coffee shop enjoying the sun and resting.

Plan Your Day

Yes, plan your day the night before. Don't waste your best brain time on deciding what is actually important to get done in your day. Use it to do the tasks that matter. Remember, we are at our best shortly after we wake up. Using that time to decide what you're going to do instead of doing your important work is criminal.

Close down your work 15 minutes early at the end of the day. Look over your day and the tasks that you had originally planned to do in the week. Which tasks fit into tomorrow? Which meetings do you have?

I take a look at the client I'm planning on working for the next day and then look at Trello (my project management system) to see what tasks are on the deck for the day. I will then write down enough information in my notebook to ensure that I can work on the task without needing to dive back in to Trello to do the work.

While your project management system is a much more limited inbox than an email inbox, it is still a place where your client can add a bunch of trivial items that will distract you from pushing the project forward. By not jumping in to the project management system until I've done some work I ensure that I've done something to move the project forward.

I essentially outline the work I'm going to do for my clients the day before I do it so I don't have to spend the same amount of time getting my brain in the right thinking space for the project the next day.

When it comes to my writing work I do the same thing. The section on planning your day was fully outlined with the main ideas and links to the research I wanted to reference before I started writing today. I did that by ending my writing session yesterday 15 minutes early and writing the outline for the next piece of writing. Then when I sat down today all I had to do was start to follow the very detailed outline. I did not spend my initial writing time trying to figure out what to write, I got writing.

While it only takes me 15 minutes now to plan my days, leave yourself 30 when you're getting started. As with everything, we just don't know the exact process we'll want to use as we get started. It will take you a bit to turn the planning process into something that is automatic.

By being intentional with your planning you can turn that unproductive day in to a well organized productive day so that you can spend time executing on the good creative work that you want to be doing. More time spent executing your purpose will mean you feel so much better about your day and the progress you've made.

That's going to let you build on momentum and keep that ball rolling.

You should now have a plan to get your week under control. If you don't have that plan, stop and do the weekly planning work I just told you about. That doesn't mean that your day is going to be all daisies and roses though.

Distractions will creep in if you let them. You will have other things that try to draw you away from the most crucial work you could be doing. We're going to address these distractions next. I'm going to walk you through why you need to change the relationships you have with your devices so that you can get your highly valuable work done. I'm going to show you how to reset communication expectations with those around you so that they don't bring distractions to you.

Share Your Time Blocking

Once you've done your weekly time block, take a picture and share it. Tag it with #theartoffocus on Instagram, Twitter or Mastodon and I'll pick one image a month for a FREE coaching session with me.

7

THE WORLD WANTS TO DISTRACT YOU

No matter how much you want to focus, almost nothing around us wants to help us do that. There are kids, one of mine has been in the office 3 times in the last 20 minutes, and family and the dump truck going by. Then there is all the notifications and social media things that want to steal our attention away from the solid purpose driven work we should be doing.

This chapter is going to help you get a handle on that. It's going to help you make new relationship deals with your distractions so that you can get your valuable work done.

Cal Newport has a theory about what he calls Attention Capital. Newport says that the primary capital in the economy today is the brain's ability to create value through sustained attention. It is only through sustained attention that we can create the art, writing, code, and products that will define the world in which we live.

It's only through focused attention that we can bring the most value to our businesses and clients in the form of making smart decisions.

That means we can't be haphazard with the environments we work in. We can't blindly use any tools that come along because they might maybe have some benefit to us. We must be intentional about how we configure our workspaces and the tools we use to get our work done.

Let's dive in to what it means to be intentional about our choices in how we work.

Your Computer and Devices

For quite some time now the defacto method of getting work done in many industries has been the computer. It sits on your desk, or your lap, and you tap away on it sending missives to others or writing code or moving pixels around.

While these devices were revolutionary when they came out, we are also blindly accepting that they provide the best way to do all of our work. Entire companies are set up around the applications that are exclusively available to traditional computer environments, without ever questioning if they are still the best way to produce high quality work.

Access and response expectations are set based on a device with the option to overlap windows or even have multiple screens available to the end user.

Embrace Constraints

Before you dive in to the rest of this it's time to ask yourself, is this really the best way for you to work? I was once a person with three monitors. I loved the productivity benefits of being able to see my code on one screen, my reference material on another, and then have a third one for whatever else seemed to be the best option.

But that's changed. I'm now doing 90% of my work on an iPad Pro 9.7" and it's helped me write more words. I've delivered more code to clients. I suffer from less distraction when I'm being "productive."

The best example of that for me was yesterday. I had my computer on for a video call because I wanted to use my fancy wireless headset. Instead of reconfiguring my desk to use my iPad after the call, I stuck with the big screen and the laptop. Yes, I got some tasks done, and yes some of them were easier on the traditional desktop, but I also spent a bunch of time checking out Slack as we talked about interesting TV to watch.

I spent more time checking in with Twitter. I had to recycle myself back to my project management system to see what I was even supposed to be working on because I continued to forget in the midst of distractions.

Contrast that with every afternoon for the last few months where I worked on my iPad Pro doing web development. Yes there are some slowdowns compared to a desktop environment, but I almost never dipped into Twitter. I scheduled some time to check Slack and never kept flipping back to it to see if there was some discussion that was happening that could distract me from the task at hand. I didn't have to keep checking in with my PM tool to see what on earth I was supposed to be working on. I remembered because I didn't choose three other distractions on the way to accomplishing a task.

The constraints of iOS have meant that when I say I'm working, I am in fact spending all my attention on the tasks that I should be focused on.

In their excellence book Switch, Chip and Dan Heath talk about the need to shape the path of decisions. They say:

> What looks like a people problem is often a situation problem.

They're telling us that it's not that people are choosing bad things, but that the situations they are in are built to facilitate the bad decisions. The multi-windowed environment that a desktop allows is built to have many things around. At one point we said that it was great because multitasking was great, but we know it's not.

While studies have shown that people get more work done with multiple screens, they all seem contrived to me. Who can't help but get more work done in a controlled setting when your choice is to look at reference material on one screen and type it in on another.

That doesn't represent any of the work environments I see anyone working in.

People don't work in a laboratory. They work in open offices. They work in coworking spaces or libraries or at home with kids making noise downstairs. These are all environments that have distractions on top of the distractions that they can bring to themselves with all manner of messaging clients, email, and social media.

My goal every day is to write well. To dig into topics deeper than the typical blogger. To spend my afternoons focused on getting solid work done for clients. My goal is not to check in on 27 different messaging clients or to be blindly enticed by some social algorithm into giving away my nonrenewable time.

So I choose iOS because it helps me make better decisions about where I direct my focus.

What is Best for You?

Now, what is best for you? What is your goal every day? Where do you provide the most value? What physical tools, software, and work spaces facilitate that for you?

Note that I'm starting by focusing on you. We're not asking what's best in the eyes of those around you. Heck those people around you are nice. They may even like you and be tempting you with things that seem like they're good for you.

A friend of mine recently got me invited to a Facebook group. He did it because he thought that I could contribute to the group and get some coaching clients. It was done with only the thought to help me have a business that has more income. While I appreciate the effort, Facebook is freaking terrible and I stay as far away from it as possible.

It rarely has anything I want to look at. It's mostly full of groups and people I don't have any reason to interact with. So I declined the invite and continued to rarely use Facebook despite the huge compliment of being invited to a group that likely does have some clients in it for me.

Take a look at each device you have, what is your computer for in your eyes? What is your tablet or phone for? Is your phone for calls and text messages or social media? If it's for calls and text messages, why on earth do you have Instagram on it?

Do you have those social media applications on there because you feel some obligation that "this is where people are"? That's not a good enough reason.

As I've left different groups, I've had people get annoyed. They lament the fact that I don't answer Facebook messages. I've had an email about it which amounted to telling me that it was easier for them to use Facebook so I better interact in a manner they found easiest.

Once you've started to look at what brings the most value in your work, start asking yourself what the expectations of others have caused you to do. Where are you simply following without any evaluation about the value that the software or tool provides for you?

We're going to dig much deeper in to designing your devices for focus shortly and the whole next chapter is about building an environment that makes it easy to get the best work possible from you.

Getting Focused with Your Computer

Before we dive in to getting focused with your desktop, remember the first question to ask yourself is "what is this device for?"

A good second question is: "How does this device cause me to bring less value to my work?"

You can use a bunch of tricks to make a device more compatible with your value, but they're hacks. The whole process of getting more focused work done starts with you and the choices you make.

Yes, most of my work is done on iOS now, but there are pieces that I do on macOS. Specifically audio recording is done with my computer. In fact, most video and audio conferencing seems to be easier on macOS where I can have a video call up and still reference notes.

So that means my laptop is a video and audio machine and doesn't need anything else on it. When I realized this, I removed a whole bunch of things I could possibly use to do work. With less choices about the work I could do, I stay focused on the tasks I intend to focus on when I sat down at my computer.

Look at your computer and decide what it's for. Is it a gaming device? Do you need to write on it? Do you really need social media clients on it or are they part of the list of things that cause you to bring less value to your work?

To get a proper clean slate to work from, do a full backup and then reinstall your operating system. Below are the tools you and tutorials you need to do this on Windows and macOS.

- Clone macOS with SuperDuper
- Reinstall macOS
- Acronis to Clone on Windows
- Reinstall Windows

Now you've got that clean slate to work with. Write down on a sticky note or piece of paper what the machine you're looking at is for. Yes, I said write it down as in with a pen. Keep that handy as you're working with your computer.

If your computer is a writing machine, then install your writing software. If you need to do email with it, then sure install an email client. If Twitter is always a problem, then don't install a client for it and use Self Control (macOS) or Cold Turkey (Windows and macOS) to block the site entirely.

Both of these option let you set timers, so that you're blocked from the problematic sites for the desired amount of time. Cold Turkey allows you to schedule when things are blocked so that you can build a routine around when you should be working, and when it's okay to have some distraction around.

Outside of the few basic things you must install to make your computer functional, leave everything else alone. Spend the next week only installing applications that must be installed. At the end of the week what has been installed? It's likely that these are the only things you need on your computer to do most of your work.

If you followed along, you've now built a device that is ready for your work. Keep that note around. Every time you look at installing something new on your computer, pull it out again to ask yourself if it really enhances the work that your computer was designed for.

If it doesn't don't install it. You're only installing a distraction from the maximum value you can produce.

Getting Focused with iOS or Android

For iOS (or Android) you've got the same first two questions, what is the device for and how does it cause you to bring less value to your work. Really there are two classes here, your phone and any other tablet device. They can each be treated differently and set up for different tasks.

I have my tablet setup as my main work machine focused on writing and building content. My phone is a phone and has Instagram on it because I do like to post photos. Before my iPad was the main work device I had Instagram on my iPad so that it was not always in my pocket.

Now that my iPad is my main device Instagram is a distraction so it got removed and added to my phone. To stop myself from checking it on my phone I made the rule that if there is any other option my phone doesn't go in my pocket. In the car it is in the door. When I have my backpack with me, it's in the phone pocket. When I'm at home it's on top of the fridge or in the charging drawer we have at the house.

Note I describe rules. I did not talk about my intention. I didn't say to myself "oh I need to just stop checking Instagram" I created a new rule around my phone. We're much less likely to violate a rule. So don't set intentions, make rules to keep you away from the behaviours you don't want to participate in.

I followed the same process with my phone and tablet. I wiped them and then wrote down what they were for. I installed the main applications I'd need on them and then I left them alone. After a week they had all the applications I needed to get stuff done.

For my tablet, I made sure that I kept iMessage off the device. It's not there to be a messaging device, it's there to be a writing and research tool.

My phone is for phone calls, Instagram, podcasts and messaging with friends and family. That means I have no work messaging applications on it. Slack is on my iPad only and all the notifications are turned off. I do nothing "emergency" in my work so no one needs to get in touch with me right away. I can deal with any Slack messages or other messages during my scheduled message time.

You may not be able to do that, but you surely don't need instant notification from every possible channel that you have. Every Slack channel is not important. Most Twitter messages are on crucial. 99% of your email, can wait a few hours. Let it all wait.

There is still one tablet device I haven't talked about, my Kindle Paperwhite. Yes I could use my iPad as a reading device or my iPhone as a reading device, and sometimes I do. The thing is that they also offer other distractions when I could be reading books. That makes a Kindle a great device for reading, while being terrible at allowing me any other type of distraction. Even surfing the Amazon store that's built in or Goodreads is less than desirable on the Kindle, so I just read.

It's all about using the right tool to help you stay on task with your most valuable work. Choose the right tool and then make sure you shape the choices you can make with the device so that you only do the work that you should be doing.

Choosing not to change your relationship with your devices means that you are choosing distraction. You are choosing to be less productive, to bring less value to your work. If that's the choice you want to make, I guess that's fine.

I don't think you're reading this book because that's the type of choice you want to make though.

Resetting Communication Expectations

I mentioned that I don't put iMessage on my iPad, but I've taken my dislike of interruptions further by putting my phone in Do Not Disturb mode all the time and setting a VIP list. My list is short, really short. In fact the only way that my phone rings is if my wife calls me from her phone. It doesn't even make a noise when she sends me a text message.

Most of our text messaging is not urgent. She's venting about something silly our kids did, or asking me to get milk on the way home. I can read either of those when I'm done working and respond to them then. They do nothing in the moment they are sent except steal my focus from the work at hand.

If there is truly an emergency that I need to know about, then she can call me and it would get through. Everything else can wait.

I didn't just do this to my phone without talking to my wife. She was aware that I'd be changing my phone settings and that sometimes she wouldn't get a reply from me as soon as she sent me a text. She is aware that the only way to get in touch with me right away is to call.

Before you can make any big changes in who can interrupt you, you need to make sure that you've set expectations properly.

One time when my in-laws were visiting my father-in-law continued to bring my oldest kid up to the office to "say hi" to dad. Yes I love my kids, but constant interruptions are death to getting any good work done. I ended up telling him to go away and he was annoyed that I didn't "want to see my daughter."

Later on we had a better discussion about giving my focus time during work hours. He had never really thought about the focus I need to have because I work at home. By focusing now later I could spend time with my daughter without feeling like work was hanging over my head. Once we had changed the expectations, I only got called when there was a true first step or word.

As you look at who can access you, make sure you evaluate

everyone on your list. Do they all need to get in touch with you right away? Can some wait for days, or weeks, to get a response from you?

Don't feel bad about letting some people sit. Your goal every day should be to do the work that brings the most value to your business. Your goal with every relationship should be to engage with people that bring the most value to you.

Let the other people wait.

We've just covered how to reset a bunch of your relationships. You should have reset how you use your computers and devices. You should have a good handle on resetting the communication expectations that others have for you.

But there is another step coming. Next we're going to look at how you can design the environment around you to make sure that you have the highest chance of staying focused on your high value work.

I'm going to walk you through some of the cues that have helped me stay focused on my work so that I bring high value to every hour I'm in my office.

8

DESIGNING YOUR ENVIRONMENT
FOR FOCUS

When I surveyed my readers one of the things they said distracted them the most was the floor plan of their office. A number of them worked in open plan offices, and they said that the distraction this caused killed their productivity. They said it was full of other people being loud, and constant interruptions from coworkers.

Recently there have even been some small scale studies that say that open offices don't accomplish the task they were intending to solve. Far from promoting collaboration and "synergy" they cause people to draw deeper in to themselves and rely only on digital tools like Slack to communicate. That means they encounter more distractions in the small emails and messages they get pinged with daily. They rarely get to focus.

Unfortunately, we don't all have the option of building our ideal offices. My ideal office sits over a large garage which is totally separate from my house. There is a full shower there and a suite for when family visits, but the suit doesn't connect directly to my office.

I have a comfortable reading space, and a couch and even a TV for the nights that the parents want to have a date but don't really want to leave the house while the kids are watched. My office would have a bunch of windows that look out over trees and some open space.

I have a little corner that is set up as a recording studio so that I can have reasonably clean audio. My desk has a space for my main digital work device (iPad or whatever) and a good space to go analogue with my notebooks.

Right now, my work space is nothing like that. I have a desk for my computer that I shift around as I've been moving more towards an iPad Pro as my main device. My kids are currently having a lively "discussion" outside the door and my bed is just behind me. While I was editing this section my middle child was playing with Lego on the bed and getting me to fix the items she pulled apart by accident.

Yes I can change my desk from sitting to standing height, but at the end of the day it always needs to be set to standing height so that the temptation to mess with it is reduced for my young children.

My other office is one of the local coffee shops. There is a fair bit of noise in these, which I try to negate with a decent set of headphones. My current choice is a set of Jaybird Freedom 2 wireless headphones mainly because their small and they can run all day as I cycle the external battery pack off and on the main headphones between charge cycles.

Another great option is the Bose Quiet Comfort 35. These are bigger to carry around but they have active noise cancelling which will mean that you are much less distracted by the ambient noise in the environments you are in.

While the coffee shop can be a great space to work, it can also be terrible. You can never predict what will be going on or who will be having some socially awkward fight in the coffee shop. Test out the options nearest you because it may be the case that going an extra few minutes will provide a place much more suited to work.

Despite the drawbacks you may have with your current workspace, there is much you can do to ensure that when you're working, you're achieving a high degree of effective focused work.

Choose Your Workspace

Both CPG Grey and Austin Kleon have different desks in their office for different types of work. Kleon has two different desks. One is setup for his artistic analogue work and the other is set up for his computer based work.

CPG Grey has an office at home for recording. He has a remote office with two different desks. One for script writing and one for video editing and animation.

We've already talked about this, but it's so crucial to success I want to cover it again. Cal Newport has something he calls Attention Capital Theory. This is the idea that the biggest value now is our brain's ability to create new ideas and value through sustained attention. While some of us like Kleon and Grey have the means to tailor an office for this, most of us don't.

That doesn't mean we can't take steps towards making ourselves more effective through our workspaces.

The first changes you can make in your working space is to decide which type of work is best suited to the available spaces you have. Your home office may be best suited to coding work and you may find that moving to the coffee shop helps you write better.

I find that working a few hours in the morning at my house and then changing locations to a local coffee shop or library provides a huge boost to my productivity. The break of a few hours while I run or hang out with my kids, combined with the new location means that my brain feels ready to dig deep into the creative well again.

A Clean Workspace

While I love a clean desk, my wife has always done her best work with a messy work space. Though she does have a hard time finding things from time to time.

There is an interesting study out there that says in the midst of chaos, we look for any goals that bring order to our lives. The problem is that when we sit in the midst of disorder, we can easily pursue any goal at all without regard to how it contributes to the main goal we have.

With clutter around, are you more likely to try and tidy a bit instead of working on the writing project at hand? Are you updating your website instead of writing code for your client site?

For that reason, at least try wiping your desk clean and starting over with a clean work space. How do you feel when you enter it? Does the lack of clutter help you focus? Are you getting in to creative flow easier? Are you making progress towards the main goals that matter more often?

Yes, you'll need to have some measurements like productive time or words written or code shipped, to use as you try a clean desk surface. Start measuring now, and plan to clean up the office in two weeks. Then measure again over the next few weeks and see what you need in your office for tidiness to get the most work done.

Set Your Cues

Once you've done what you can with the space you have, it's time to set your cues and routines to help you work optimally. There is a balance to hold here though. If you build a routine that's too rigid then the slightest change can throw you off and you'll be getting no work done.

The goal is to build a number of flexible cues as starting points to help you fall in to the flow you need for your work.

My morning starts with heading up to my office and putting on my headphones. The music doesn't matter much to me, though many people need music without words to focus. I like something with a bit of a beat. You may even catch me singing along with the song if I know it.

After that, I don't need anything outside of the iPad/computer I'm using for work. The only cue that really helps me fall in to creative flow is those headphones and music. You'll even find me at home with no one around using the headphones at the kitchen table in the midst of a kitchen that isn't quite so neat. With the headphones and some music, I'm able to focus and get work done.

This cue is easy to take with me. At the library or the coffee shop I put my headphones on and feel like it's time to get down to work.

What is it for you? Do you need a cup of coffee in your hand? Do you need to have the right chair? Do you need quiet? Make sure you test what helps you get in to creative flow and then optimize your environment so that you can have those cues.

On the other side of this is the things you don't want to have happen. The things that block your creativity or steal your time. As with many people, that's email or social media for me. I don't check either of them until late in the day. In fact, the only day I work to clear out my email is Friday.

On Friday I'm between coaching calls all day. The only thing I can do between calls is to answer an email or two. Friday I try to clear out my inbox but every other day of the week I may not even check email.

Do you need to make sure that your main task for the day is written out? How about start your day with email and social media blocked?

Multi-Screen Setups

While there is some research saying that multi-screen setups win in productivity, I remain unconvinced. I remain sceptical because the research I've seen so far is contrived.

Sure give people a set of tasks that require a bunch of windows open and when they can see more windows, they do the task faster. What they're not taking in to account is all the random crap that people fill their extra screens with.

Twitter is sitting over there barely out of site. As is Slack and Quora, and a whole host of other things that are not the task at hand.

When I am taking people backpacking I always tell them that whatever size bag they own is the size they'll fill. They will keep finding stuff that will fit in the bag and stuff that they must have for the trip.

In my experience, we fall in to this with multi-screen setups as well. We have empty screen space so we fill it. We see that second or third screen hanging out beside us, so we glance at it instead of staying focused on the task at hand.

Yes, multiple screens make multitasking easier, but multitasking is broken and you shouldn't be doing it.

As I said in the previous section, I went from a three screen setup to a single iPad Pro 9.7" and increased my focus time. More words written, more code shipped all in less time. I've taken my desktop from a three screen setup to a single large screen and even there, get more focused work done with less distractions because there is nothing hanging around to steal my attention.

Setting up your environment to not steal your attention is as important as setting it up for productivity. Make sure you don't ignore the things that can take away from your focus as you build cues to help you get in creative flow.

Now that you're done, make sure you schedule time on your calendar to wipe your workspace clean and build one that is ready for your focus. You have a solid plan for some of the cues that will help you stay focused with your work. You know some of the steps you have to take to build those cues in to your routines so that it becomes second nature to drop in to focus mode.

That still presents a problem for some of you though, because you don't control your whole day. You work a job and your boss decides what your office environment looks like.

Well we're about to cover that for you. In the next chapter I'm going to tell you how to work with your boss so that you can focus on the highest value work that you do. By doing this, you can free up more time to push your main focus forward.

9

FINDING FOCUS WHEN YOU WORK FOR SOMEONE ELSE

So far we've firmly focused at those of us that control our own time. Those of us that can decide to get up and start work at 5am, because we set our schedule. What if your family just doesn't allow that? What if your job doesn't make that possible?

I had a boss that would get mad if I'd come in an hour early to leave an hour early. They didn't care about the amount of work I'd get done before everyone showed up, they only cared that I was there during the hours they were.

There was no meetings I was missing, we really had no meetings. They just wanted to make sure that they could see me in my chair when they wanted me there. That meant that I'd often show up early after dropping my wife at her office and then I'd start work early and work a "full day" before surfing the internet sitting in my chair until I was allowed to leave the building and go pick my wife up from work.

Talk about a waste of my time and the company resources. I dealt with that job by leaving, because the scenario above was only one small piece of a puzzle that had lots of terribleness in it.

Build Some Career Capital First

If that sounds something like what you deal with the place to start as you look at getting focus in your workplace is building some career capital. I first heard about this idea from Cal Newport in So Good They Can't Ignore You. Here is how he puts it:

> To construct work you love, you must first build career capital by mastering rare and valuable skills, and then cash in this capital for the type of traits that define compelling careers.

If you're just starting in a career, or at a workplace, you may not be able to affect change in the organization. You're just starting and you still need to prove yourself. If that's you start by doing your best to show that by prioritizing focus you'll get more work of value done.

I've found that once you've been able to show you're getting more valuable work done managers are enthusiastic about the idea. With some career capital behind you, it's easier to move on to the suggestions in the rest of this section.

So to start, implement the few things from the previous chapters of the book that you can. Develop your cues to help you get in to focus mode. Shut your email down, and plan your day the night before so that you start by getting focused good work done.

As you'll see shortly, I've always been the type of person that bucks the rules and does what he thinks is right. While this has paid off, it's also made my road much harder. Build some career capital, then dig in with your employer to get them on your side so that the whole company can get more focus.

Find Where You Bring Most Value

For every job, there are the core value tasks you were hired for, and then there are the rest of the things that you end up getting bogged down in. Most of us assume that we have to participate in these other things, because everyone else does, but you don't.

In my first web development job I was the last one in the door on the team for a year. I was just out of college and had little real world experience in building websites. Yet, I was the one that didn't end up in meetings. I was the one that didn't get interrupted. I was the one that after a year was making more than everyone but my boss.

I was also the only one that wasn't complaining about getting interrupted. I was the only one not expected work evenings and weekends to catch up on my areas of responsibilities.

All this was a result of a talk I had with my boss in my first month. That talk detailed the three things that I did to provide the most value to the company. With that list in hand, I started tracking my time and sent my boss a quick summary of it every week. That summary detailed the roadblocks I had hit as I tried to focus on my three value areas.

It only took two weeks and my boss was in knocking down any blocks I had in my focus. Unfortunately for the rest of the developers I worked with, it didn't transfer to them because they were happy enough with the status quo.

That's where getting focus in your work starts. You need to have a value conversation with your boss. Tell them you want to talk about how you can bring more value to the team. Be clear that it's not a talk about getting a raise.

Give them your short list of the things you think bring the most value to the team ahead of the meeting. This way they can look at it instead being blindsided by the idea during the meeting. Ask them to verify or change the items that bring the most value to the team. This way you can both be on the same page.

With your three value areas defined, ask your boss how much time you should be spending on these things. Use a percentage approach. Should you be spending 80% of your time on these things? What about 90% or 70%? Get your boss to commit to a number.

It doesn't matter what the number is to start. Sure we'd love it if our boss said 90%, but they may say 50%. It's okay to try and point them towards a higher number for your focus time, but don't make a big fight about it.

Once you know the amount of time you should be spending or your areas of value, start tracking your time so that you can provide a report to your boss every week showing how much of your time you spent on these three areas.

Make sure you detail how much time you spent in things that don't directly contribute to the core value areas you have. Are you dealing with emails that you shouldn't be? Even deleting endless CC chains takes time away from the value you can provide to your job. Are you being asked to jump in to Slack every 10 minutes because that's the company expectation?

What most people find when they go through this exercise with their boss is that their boss had never thought about the core value focus. They had never realized how much time got spent on things that were not bringing value to the organization. They loved the idea of less email and fast access in Slack, but they didn't realize how much interruption it facilitated.

When my coaching clients have done this, we've seen wholesale changes in how things run because someone finally made the company look at how much time they were wasting on tasks that provided little, or no value to the organization. They assumed that there was more time spent on high value items than there was.

Forcing Decisions

The second big thing I did with my boss was to force decisions about what my priorities were. As with most jobs, stuff came up in the course of the days and weeks at work. My boss or another developer would come by my desk with some extra task. I'd always agree to do it on one condition, that my supervisor indicate which of my priority tasks did not have to get done so I'd have time for the extra item.

They never picked the new task. They always wanted me to stay focused on the tasks that were a priority and had been assigned weeks ago. This meant at the end of every sprint I'd have everything off my list done and tested, where most of my colleagues had some stuff done but never all.

When new tasks cone up, force the decision. Don't blindly do the work. Make it clear that the new task will take away from the items that you have established as priority work. In most cases there was not thought put in to how adding a task would affect the highest value items.

All my focused work meant that I was the one with raises and promotions because I was always the one with all my tasks done. I was also the only one with almost nonexistent overtime.

Developing Focus in a Team

It's all well and good for you to get focus time, but it's even better if you can make focus time something your whole team can get regularly. There are two methods you can use to approach this.

First, and the one I like the most, is core focused hours. This is choosing a set of hours in the day where the whole office agrees it's time to focus. No office visits. No expectations on email response. Internal chat is muted. You just work.

A good model is to start the day with focus. Say 8-11 is all about focus. Then use 11-2 for meetings and a more regular office. Use the end of the day for more focused time.

Don't let any meetings happen inside focus led work time. Be rigid with it until the whole office has established the habit of focused work.

The second way to work with a team on focus is to decide on a single visible indicator. At my first development job I had this going for me as well. See I was the only one pushing focus as the thing we should be doing. Everyone else was down with the normal office interruption culture.

To combat this I bought a huge set of headphones. No one could say they didn't see me wearing them. I'd put them on during the times I wanted to focus on my work as a single visible marker that I was focused on the task at hand. I'd even make a point of not reacting if someone called my name from across the room. They'd have to come get in my line of sight to interrupt me.

What I found was, that as I stuck to the single measure of focus people stopped interrupting me. They'd still call my name from across the office, but then they'd see the headphones and not follow up because they knew I was focused on the task at hand.

When the headphones came off, I made a point of being highly responsive to any requests for my time. I picked my own "core" focus hours so I was predictable. The requests for my input just naturally started to only come outside of my focus hours.

It doesn't have to be headphones, but choose a single identifiable thing that shows you're focusing. Maybe it's chat status, or a note on the back of your chair where one side says "STOP". Make it consistent and when you're focusing raise the bar a bit for people to interrupt you.

Establish Levels of Access

One of the final ways that you can do better at focus on a team is to establish levels of access for the communication channels that are used in the team.

Most teams have a number of communication types. You can email people, or use the project management systems. You can stop by someone's desk, or use the chat application that your team prefers.

Unfortunately, some teams only have a single method of communication, the all encompassing company chat. The problem with this is that every communication request is treated with equal priority. You get pinged for anything, and you just have to respond to it.

Some of that communication can wait for hours. In fact, most of it can wait for hours. But since it's all in one spot you can never differentiate between what needs to be dealt with now and what can wait.

Make sure you have at least two different methods of communication in your team so that you can establish different response times. Make sure that you're clear about the response times for each medium across the team so that everyone is on the same page.

Let's explore what I mean assuming you have email a project management system and Slack as your communication channels.

With these three options for communication you can establish that emails get answered within a few days. The PM system is within 24 hours and Slack is answered right away, outside core focus hours. In fact, make sure that no one is expected to be on Slack inside focus hours because it's an easy way to get some distraction in and look busy.

> If you send and answer e-mails at all hours, if you schedule and attend meetings constantly, if you weigh in on instant message systems like Hall within seconds when someone poses a new question, or if you roam your open office bouncing ideas off all whom you encounter — all of these behaviours make you seem busy in a public manner. - Deep Work

By establishing the length of time that you are expected to respond in a team you can give people freedom to find the focus they need and ignore the communication channels that just don't matter in the moment. This also means that you can choose the proper method of communication and reduce irritation when you don't get a response as fast as you had hoped.

Communication speed is also about expectation matching. If you send an email and expect a response in an hour, but the person you sent it to only looks at email once a day, you may be in for a frustrated surprise when you don't get a response in that hour.

Just like it's not fair for others to expect you to use their communication channels in they way they prefer, it's no okay for you to expect others to respond based on how you use your communication tools. Like my friend that was mad at me for not using Facebook Messenger so he could get in touch with me quickly. I'm not on Facebook Messenger, and that's his problem. He takes forever to reply to any text messages from me, and that's my problem.

I'm okay with waiting. I never send him a communication via text that I need a fast response on. If I need him right away, I call his phone because he answers it. I don't love talking on the phone, but I choose the communication channel appropriately based on how quickly I need a response.

When you establish a set of expectations in a team, everyone has the freedom to choose the best method of communication for the information they need. Everyone's expectations are set properly. You can save loads of frustration, and get more productivity in your team with proper expectations.

I've already talked about assigning different response priority to different people, so remember you can apply that filter here as well. An email from your top priority client should get a response sooner than much of the rest of your email. Let the rest sit, and don't worry about it.

You should now have a good idea of how to set better expectations around communication channels and how to define high priority tasks with your boss. You should have a good handle on your time. You should have an environment that is built for focused work. You should be on a path towards doing your most vital work if you have a job and you can then leverage that in to purchasing more of your time.

Now that we have more effective time, we can move on to testing our ideas. Not just testing them against what we want, but doing the research in the market to understand fully what our customers want. Part III will give you the tools you need to test your ideas in the market so that you can keep taking steps towards living your passion.

PART III

PART III: TESTING YOUR IDEAS

10

IF YOU'RE NOT INTENTIONAL IT WON'T HAPPEN

I started this book by telling you that you'd get the exact systems that I use for my business. The systems and practices I use to make sure I have time to focus. The way I plan my day so that I can get thousands of words written in a day and still ship code to clients. The systems I use so that by 3pm I can hang out with my kids, after taking a few hours off in the middle of the day for myself.

I wasn't always like that though. When I started running my own business I was banking on the benevolent universe. I was like Linus longing for The Great Pumpkin. I figured that if I was just earnest enough then everything I produced would win in the market.

It didn't happen like that. One day in particular I remember taking my wife on a "drive date" where I just happened to remember that we were near a client who had a cheque for me. We picked it up and stopped by the bank and then with that deposited I could actually pay us for the month.

I didn't fool her. She was just very gracious and played along with my game.

In the first section of the book we worked through what we want our life to look like. We built some strong filtering documents that we can use to test our ideas against so that we don't end up with work that we hate.

Next, I walked you through how you build focused work time in to your life whether you work for yourself or you work at a traditional job. When you can maximize your effective time you can have the space to work on your next big idea.

This section is all about vetting and testing the ideas you have. Simply floundering around isn't going to work any more than random chance. Expecting that some cosmic deity of goodness will smile down on your idea and bless you because you're the most earnest is a recipe for failure.

You have to have some sort of plan if you want to maximize your chances at success. You have to stop idolizing the lone creative that creates and does no testing and marketing and still lucks in to success. While the world likes to write stories about that single success, it's a single success in a vast field of the corpses of the dreams of other creatives. These dreams died long before any traction happened.

Are you ready to learn to talk like your prospects and build traction for your ideas so that you can build the business you've been dreaming of? That's what Part III of The Art of Focus is all about.

11

UNDERSTANDING HOW YOUR PROSPECTS TALK ABOUT THEIR PROBLEMS

You've already got your ideas filtered down to the top 1 - 3 that seem like they have the most promise. These ideas made it through your filtering documents. If you can work hard on one and turn it into something that wins, then you'll have earned that life you want.

Now it's time to start turning these ideas into reality. This process starts by figuring out how your prospects talk about their problems. Without knowing how your prospects talk about the problem you're trying to solve, you won't be able to sell effectively to them. You won't be able to build a compelling product because you won't be talking about it in the ways your prospects talk about it.

This chapter will show you how to research your prospects so that you can fully understand what it is they value and how they talk about their problems.

It's possible that after this step you'll realize that one or all of your ideas is not going to work. It's also possible that you'll find a problem that is so much more painful than the ones you thought of.

Don't get discouraged in either case. Take any new ideas and run them back through your filtering documents out of section one. Evaluate them again and see if they match up with where you want to go.

If you've eliminated all your ideas, then head back to the first section of the book and go through the idea generation process again. You have more knowledge now. You will likely have a bunch of new ideas from your research.

Now, let's start digging deeper in to the challenges we want to solve.

Do Some Research

You're going to need to start a blank document of some sort. A Word file or spreadsheet is best. You can also turn to the third section of the workbook where I've provided spots to fill in this research.

Defining the Right Questions

The place to start as you're working to understand how your prospects are talking about the problems they have is Quora. Quora is a question and answer site. It has hundreds of thousands of questions and even more answers. This is the best place to start because it has people inside your target market asking questions about the problems they're having.

I use this as a resource all the time as I'm looking for new content ideas for books and blog posts. When I have a new product I want to develop I start with Quora to see how people are asking questions that revolve around the problem.

Most of these people will have spent time searching online using the exact same language they've used in their question. Nothing relevant enough came up, so they're looking to Quora to get the answer they want.

Start by finding relevant groups to the ideas you have. Then look through the questions being asked. Are any of the questions ones that could be answered by your product or service? Write down the exact wording of the questions that are relevant.

Make sure you also look at the answers. What services or products are being recommended? Does your solution make any of the suggestions on Quora easier? Can you solve the same problem faster or better than what has been suggested? Are any suggestions direct competitors to what you're developing?

Write all of that information down. Don't assume you're going to remember which products were competitors.

Then use the search functionality on Quora to search for other questions that are relevant to your idea. Do you see any repeat questions? Are there any repeat services? Are there any people consistently answering questions? Make sure you track their names for later reference.

Who Else Is Solving the Problem?

Now that we have a list of questions that have been asked by the potential customers you have for your idea, it's time to take those questions and start searching wider on the web for possible solutions.

Let's start with blogs. You can use "blog: $keyword" to limit your searches in Google to blogs that are relevant to your keyword. Make sure you use the exact questions that you drummed up in Quora.

You should make note of any products or services that you find here as well. Also watch for the authors of the posts you find or the owners of the sites. Are you seeing any repeat names? Write those names down.

Look through the people that have commented on the posts too. Make note of any commenters that provided good additional content. We'll come back to the names later. For now they can be great resources for you to reach out to so that you can talk about your idea and get some feedback.

People love being contacted as the "expert". In almost every case they'll be willing to talk to you further about what you're doing and they'll likely offer insights that you miss.

Next up is forums. We're going to tackle them in about the same way. Use the search "forum: $keyword" to search for forums that deal with your problem. Again, make sure that you use the exact phrasing of the questions out of Quora. You can even use them in the search that is found on the forums.

When you get to forums, also search the words "help" and "problem". Some of the posts will be general help in using the software, but a bunch will be problems that people are having inside the niche you want to serve. Do these problems line up with any of the ideas that you have?

As you search through forums, make note of the brands, products, people, and solutions that are talked about. These should be added to your research sheet.

The second biggest search engine in the world is YouTube. Go to YouTube and use the keywords you did as you searched blogs and forums. Make sure you use the exact questions you found in Quora as well.

Make note of the popular videos. What people or brands or solutions are talked about? You should be seeing some repeat in these already. If you're looking at video reviews of products, what are the problems identified in them? Where do current offerings fall short? Does your idea have the potential to solve those problems?

As always, make sure you note the names of the people posting comments and videos. You're likely going to see overlap between these across different mediums.

Amazon is the biggest retailer online. Use their vast wealth of products to search for the books or resources that align with your ideas. You've likely already found some books mentioned because they were mentioned in the research you've been doing. What do these books cover?

How are the books presented? What do the 2 and 3 star reviews say? Avoid the 5 and 1 star reviews because they're either glowing or trash. It's unlikely that they'll help you. Do the reviews consistently say that there is a piece of content missing? Will your service fill that gap?

Your next research stop will be podcasts. Here you're going to use a fairly complex search outlined below.

```
"$keyword" (incontent:podcast OR intitle:pod-
cast or inurl:podcast OR inurl:episode)
```

This search is going to help you find the podcasts that deal with the problem you're going to solve. Make note of the names of the podcasts. What brands do they talk about? Which influencers do you see as guests? Which podcasts seem to have the most listenership?

Make note of all these things in your worksheet.

Out of all the research you've done you should have a long list of influencers that deal with things in and around the problem you're going to solve for clients. Plug the influencer name in to all the searches we've done so far.

How do they present themselves? What are they charging for their services? How in demand do they appear to be? What do their social profiles look like? Who do they follow?

Take notes on how they detail their solutions and how they interact with their audiences. It's likely that some keys to hitting the market right can be found inside how they present themselves.

Our final stop is going to be doing an evaluation of the solutions that we've found already. You do this by searching `review $solution`. I always find that the best reviews come from people that aren't just doing affiliate marketing. In many cases these can be noticed because they look really "polished" or they've got enough reviews to allow for multiple reviews a day.

I'd always prefer to see some random blog that gets updated a couple times a month but isn't the slickest thing on the web. Usually these are run by enthusiasts in the field. It's a hobby that they put a bunch of time in to and while it generates some side income, it's not their main line of work.

These sites always seem to be more honest about the failures of the solutions out there. For almost every product you should find some reviews that are parts good and bad. If you haven't found a wide spectrum of reviews, then keep digging because it's highly unlikely that you've found some winning perfect product.

Make note of the ways that the existing solutions don't quite match up to expectations. Does your idea fit in to this gap? How are you going to make sure that your idea doesn't have the same problem?

You should have a big list, but that doesn't mean you're done. You probably have a bunch of new names and products and ideas. If you think you've found a new problem to solve that is better than your original idea, take it back through the evaluation process from the first part of the book. Make sure it ranks above any ideas you have already. Don't just run headlong into execution.

It can be easy to get stuck in this research phase. Research feels like progress, but it's not getting any work done towards shipping your idea. Give yourself at maximum a day to do this research. If you're still going after a day, you're likely only procrastinating on the next step in making sure your idea fits in the market.

If you have another idea that comes up, or you toss the original idea, give yourself another day or two to focus down on the new thing. It could take a few weeks to get down to a single idea, but it shouldn't take months. If it's taking months, you're masking research as productivity and fooling yourself.

How is it all connected?

Dirk gently is a Holistic Detective, and yes he's fictional. What this means is that he stumbles around and things just happen to him. His catchphrase is "everything is connected" and in this fantasyland things are connected and in the end it somehow works out for him. The case is solved.

There are flying purple people eaters and alternate dimensions on the way. You don't see how things are going to fit together. It's more than a bit ludicrous, but the case gets solved in the end.

You're not a Holistic Detective. There are no energy sucking vampires to deal with people you're trying to avoid. You will not escape the flying purple people eater by jumping through the door that has old style TV static on it which allows you to exit a pocket dimension inside an abandoned house.

That means you need to sit down and figure out where your idea fits inside all of this research you've done.

Start by writing down the two or three questions you found in your research on Quora. I'm sure you found more than two or three, but usually there are a few main ones. The rest are variations on a theme. Put the main ones sticky notes on the wall or in your preferred mind mapping software.

Around those questions, place the people and solutions that serve them. It's likely that the people will have solutions that span a few of the questions.

Once you have them mapped out around the questions, it's time to step back and see how your product or service will fit in to the ones that are already out there. Is there a problem question that doesn't seem to have any solution so far? Does your idea cover that?

Are all the solutions geared to one segment of the market? Is that the only profitable segment? How can you target the other segments of the market?

We spent this chapter doing research to make sure that the ideas we move forward with have potential. I showed you the exact process I use to make sure that I'm solving a problem that real people have.

In the next chapter, we're going to talk about how to figure out how to get traction in your business because if you're not bringing new people in to your products and services, you have a hobby.

Show Me You Know How Your Prospects Talk

Take a picture of your research and share it on Mastodon, Twitter or Instagram with the hashtag #theartoffocus. I'll pick one image a month for a FREE strategy session.

12

HOW TO GET TRACTION WITH
YOUR IDEAS

Once you understand how your prospects talk about their problems, you're ready to start diving in and testing your idea in the market. You're ready to see what people are willing to pay to have you solve their problem.

In this chapter you'll find a number of ways you can use to test your ideas in the real world. No theory, just actions you can take to test your ideas and get traction so that you can take another step towards that ideal life.

Overarching Concepts for Getting Traction

Before we dive in to the specifics of getting traction with our ideas, we need to look at a few overarching principles. We've covered these already in the book, but I want to make sure that you stop again before you dive in to testing traction and make sure that you're on the right path.

There is nothing I hate more than wasting time, so I don't want to waste yours.

First, make sure you're solving real problems. Not just what you think your customers should care about, but what they actually care about. You should have discovered this as you did your research and refining of ideas. Stop again and double check that you're working on a problem people care about.

Second, make sure that you're using the language your prospects are using to describe their problems. We looked at this in the as we looked at Quora and dug through blogs and forums. If you're not sure what language to use as you test, then you didn't do the research to find out what your clients are saying. Stop, and do the research!

Third, ladder up. If you're looking at guest blogging as one of your traction channels, then you're going to have to start with the smaller blogs first. Places that are less well known. You have to earn your way in to the most popular sites. The same goes for podcasts, radio, or TV. Basically, if you want to be a guest on anything, you have to have the credibility to back it up and you need to build it first. We talked a bit about this already when we talked about career capital.

Fourth, do what you're best at. If you can write well, then it's likely that you can leverage the writing or podcasting channels best. If you struggle to get anything up on YouTube consistently, and it's vastly inferior to your competition then it's not going to be a successful channel for you. That doesn't mean you shouldn't try it, but don't just follow where everyone else is going. Do what you're good at, even if it's a bit outside of the mainstream. In fact, being just a bit off the mainstream is often a winning formula for standing out.

In her book Captivate, Vanessa Van Edwards echos this.

> The first step in winning the social game is to control the situations you play in. Only interact in places where you don't have to fake it. No matter how many behavior hacks you learn, if you go to events that make you unhappy, it will be incredibly difficult to increase your memorability. - Captivate

People can tell when you're faking it in a medium you're not good at. I'm sure that at networking events I come off as odd and not that interested. I hate networking events. I love talking to people, but I always prefer a one on one conversation where we can be honest with each other and dig deeper in to what the real problems are. You can never do this is a crowded room where you're trying to talk loud enough to be heard without yelling yourself hoarse.

Fifth, look at collaborating. You don't need to do everything alone. In fact, so many people win because they started collaborating. They gave up a bit of instant revenue and worked with someone else that could help them reach a new audience. This may mean that if you're doing a podcast, you partner with someone else that's in a similar niche. If you're bland on your own, but stand out talking to someone else you're going to attract more people in collaboration.

Sixth, don't be afraid to do unscalable stuff. Virtually everyone that buys directly from me gets a hand written card that my kids have coloured. I can't keep this up forever, but I can do it for a while. It's what is going to help me build fans for the long term.

Seventh, you need to have a measurable metric that you're aiming at. If you're looking for people on your email list so you can increase your reach then you're going to use different tactics. Specifically, going to networking events without having some sort of booth won't yield many email sign ups. If you're looking for some bigger brand recognition, then a booth at a conference may do.

You need to know what your single metric is and then test your traction channels against that metric. Stick with the one that have the biggest effect on your one metric that matters. Use any other promising ones as feeders to your single metric that matters.

Finally, don't be afraid to share everything. I used to hear that you tell people WHY they should do something and you sold the HOW. I freely admit that much of what I've written about here you can dig through the 1600 posts on my blog and find in some form or another. If people want to spend the hours amassing those posts to piece together something resembling this book, they can go right ahead. It took me around 50 hours to write this. Then another 10 to edit and package the book in to one coherent thing for you to read. It's going to take you way longer than that to find the ideas on my site, because you didn't write it all and thus don't remember the little pieces spread all over.

The same idea operates for you. Share as much as you can. People will be happy to have you help them move faster or overcome a particular challenge that they are having. The biggest problems with most ideas is that no one knows about them, not that they get ripped off.

The few people that piece together free information, were likely never going to pay you anyway.

Your One Metric That Matters

At every point in your business, you should have one metric that matters. If you're just launching your new business then it's likely your single metric is some traffic, any traffic. Any recognition of your work in the form of attention. You're just looking to get people to notice you and want to stick with you.

While you start with traffic alone, you are likely going to switch over to something like email list subscribers once you have a bit of attention. You want to be able to own the relationships that you have in your business. You want to be able to reach out to your prospects, and the best way to do this is still email.

Once you're a bit more established, then you're likely looking towards conversions to some sort of paid customer model. You're looking to take some of those people that said they were interested in what you had to say and turn them in to customers that are paying you.

Before you embark on any campaign to see what traction channel is the most effective for your business, you need to have a way to measure it. If you don't have a single metric that matters most, that you can measure, then you're wasting your time as you look at traction channels.

Don't waste your time. Identify your single metric that matters right now.

Traction Channels

You've done the work to check that your ideas have a high likelihood of winning. They're problems that people have, and you know how to speak their language. You want to solve the problem because it's going to help you build the life and business you want.

That means "all that's left" is to start telling people about the idea so that it gets traction. No I didn't say you needed to build it first because many times you don't.

When I first had the idea for this book I talked to my coaching students. Then I wrote some blog posts to see how the feedback on them went, and to make sure I had enough to say before I tackled a book.

I started to see traction in the idea of this book before I wrote the first word that was specifically for the book. I didn't even have a title for it when I started talking about it. All I had was a feeling that too many people talked about following your passion without giving you any good way to do it without spending thousands on their course.

Before you go all in on your idea, start talking about it to see if it's going to get traction in the marketplace.

Test and Refine

The first step in any work to figure out which channels are going to give you the most traction is to test them all. Put some effort in to every channel I mention here and see which one has the biggest effect.

You may find that providing a free service in trade for an email is the best way to get leads on your email list. So double down on that and using any other promising channels to feed that one which is working the best.

Don't worry about trying to do much with the channels that aren't working well right now. Don't lose focus on the single channel that is bringing in the highest benefit. Spending time with the other channels is wasted effort, unless they're being used to feed the single channel that is producing the best results.

As you test, you'll likely find that at first you have two or three promising avenues to generate leads for your new business idea. When you narrow it down to those two or three, drop the rest and start testing those two or three with a bit more effort to see which single one is the best for your business currently.

With your single biggest traction channel identified, stop focusing on the others as your main traction channel. Use them to feed the one that's making the most impact. If blogging/content is your best traction channel, this would be using ads to feed more traffic towards your content so that you increase it's impact.

Again, test the items you'll use to boost your main traction channel. Don't take for granted that Facebook ads will produce the best return. Test Facebook against any other type of traction channel and all other ad platforms you could be using and stick with the best ones only. The ones that mean the most conversion in your main traction channel. The ones that affect your single metric that matters.

You'll also find that at different times in your business, different traction channels will be the best. You may start with a campaign that is more about knowledge of your business. This may mean guest posts and guest podcast appearances are key. It may mean that getting mentioned on blogs in a PR sense is the best traction channel. But once people have some idea of who you are, you will likely need to shift your focus.

Over the life of your business, you will have to come back to your traction channels many times. Each time, start identifying the single metric that matters to you now and then testing every traction channel to see which one has the most impact on that single metric that matters.

Now, let's dive in to the traction channels that matter to small businesses.

Blogs and Content Marketing

The first step in content marketing should be using your own blog as the hub of your marketing efforts. If you want to publish content on Medium, put it on your site first and then publish it to Medium. Locking content in to Medium only means that they own your traffic. If they change how people find your content then you lose out on your readers.

This same idea would operate if you're going to do videos for YouTube. Always keep the originals and put them on your site as well. Don't just let the YouTube algorithm dictate how you get to interact with your customers.

If you're just getting started writing, then just publish. I prefer once a week as a starting publishing schedule, but it's going to be much better to go every other week and provide longer content that has higher value to your customers.

If you're just starting and are unsure how to make sure you're providing value, start with a statement like this.

"By the end of this chapter, readers will have a strategy to test the different channels they can use to gain traction so that they can test their ideas."

This is the statement I'm using for this chapter of the book. I use a statement like this for every blog post I'm going to write. In fact, it's at least in part because of a statement like the one you're reading above I'm writing this book. Every time I looked back at the original purpose of the blog post I kept knowing that it wasn't true yet. In that way one of my "test" blog posts accidentally turned in to the book you're reading.

It will take time to get notable traffic. It will take time to find your voice and find writing to be something that's easy. If you were to look at my writing output, the you might be discouraged to hear that I fairly easily write 5000 words before lunch many days a week.

Remember that I've published over 200k words as of July 2018 and 400k words in 2017. Plus I wrote and published a few books in 2017. It's because of the experience I have that I can produce written content as I do now. You need to be willing to put in the work to get there too.

If you have a blog, you also need an email list. In fact, you just need an email list no matter what traction channel you're going to use. I'm going to assume that you have an email list and that you're going to use it. At the very least send them your blog post or do a weekly round up of news that relates to the idea you're testing. Send this content round up to your list.

Once you're comfortable doing some content on your own site, it's time to look at guest posting. Here is where we start to use the laddering up strategy. If you know some people that already write in a similar niche, ask them about a guest post. Start with the smaller publications and use them as validation that your ideas have traction and that you have value to bring.

From there, move up the ladder to blogs that have bigger followings and then move up again. It make take a while, but you can get published on the top blogs in your field if you put the effort in.

If you're not sure how to approach blogs to submit guest posts when you don't know anyone at the blog, then make sure you grab the workbook to get the exact email I've used to pitch and get guest posts on many sites.

Podcasts

If you're never going to write because you hate it, then podcasting may be a better option for you. The only caveat is that audio on it's own is not something that search engines can read so you need to put some effort in to your show notes to make sure that they can bring some search traffic.

You can start a podcast with the microphone on your computer if you want. You can use your phone, and get fairly decent audio quality if you use a set of headphones with a basic microphone built in to the headphones.

Yes, there is so much more gear you can get to improve your audio quality, but it doesn't need to be perfect to get started. All it needs to be is something that your listeners can understand easily.

You can also use podcasting in conjunction with your blogging strategy, or with YouTube. I produce The Smart Business Show as an audio podcast and as a YouTube video of me as a talking head. That's one piece of content that is available in many ways and takes little extra effort on my part to produce the extra formats.

If you're just barely hanging on with writing, then maybe you should look at being a guest on podcasts. There are so many that do interviews and if you've got a bit of credibility then you can get on them. This will mean that you don't need to worry about audio production. You show up and have a fairly quiet place to record and then talk with the podcast host.

Just like with blogs, use the ladder up approach. Start with a friend as a test if they're willing. I'll have my coaching students on my podcast as a test regularly. I already know them well and can usually draw out an interesting story from them because I understand their business.

The biggest caveat to being a guest on other podcasts is that you need to have a compelling story to tell. Like I said, I have my coaching students on sometimes, but I don't do an interview show. The few interviews I've done were all about me hearing an interesting story and then wanting to share it more.

A great case in point was my talk with Adam Warner. He is a founder of FooPlugins, and after that was rolling he decided that he needed a job instead. FooPlugins was making enough money, but he needed more structure or he'd end up working all the time. Now he's a WordPress Evangelist at Sitelock. He's still a founder at FooPlugins, but his day to day is spent on Sitelock.

When you did your research earlier, you should have found a bunch of podcasts that were relevant to your industry. Head back to that list now and figure out which ones do interview shows. What types of stories are they looking for? It may not be exactly what you want to talk about, but that doesn't mean you should discount the show.

I pitched Hack The Process to talk about marketing for businesses. I'm lucky that M. David Green did a bit more research in to me because he doesn't talk at all about marketing. At least not specifically. When he replied to me he said that he doesn't talk about marketing but he did notice that I write books, blog, guest post, have a few podcasts and run a software business. He wants to talk about how I've hacked my processes to do all of that and still get to hang out with my kids.

In the midst of my conversation on Hack the Process I got to talk about my marketing book and my coaching, but it wasn't the focus. I pitched poorly to Hack The Process, and the host saved my poor pitch.

Make sure you listen to a number of episodes for each podcast you want to pitch. Take the time to understand what they want to talk about and frame your pitch in a way that shows them you understand their audience and can provide value. Even podcasts that rarely do interviews like mine, get many pitches a week asking to be on the show for some reason that has nothing to do with what I talk about.

We all just delete these emails because they are a waste of our time. Make sure you're not wasting time and make sure that you're following up.

If you're not sure what to send podcasts to pitch yourself as a guest, then make sure you download the workbook because it has the exact email sequence I use to get on podcasts.

Communities

Go back to your research and look at the different Facebook Groups and forums you found that were relevant to your idea. It's time to dig in to them and start participating. Start helping people to establish yourself as an authority.

The biggest mistake that people make here is that they start day one with lots of posts that all link back to the product they're offering. If you do this, you're likely to get kicked out as a spammer. Instead, be helpful and only mention your product or service if there is no other option. Even mention your competitor's products and talk about why their options may be better than yours. Of course, mention yours and tell people why it might be better than the competition.

At the very least, stick a link to your site in your bio because that is almost always at the bottom of every post you make. The more posts you make the more likely it is that you're going to see some traffic from the community.

I used to do a bunch of helping in the WordPress.org support forums. With one particular problem I spent the time to dig deep. It probably cost me a few hours of work time to come up with a solution and then explain to the person that needed help how to get it working on their site.

They emailed me a week later and turned in to my first $20k project. They followed that up by spending $10k a year for three years with me. Being helpful gets you traction with your idea.

Ads

Ads can be on Facebook, AdWords, paid mentions in Podcasts, posts from people like Instagram Influencers or sponsored content on sites that are relevant to your idea.

Don't be afraid to test out a new platform to see if it's going to hit an unreached segment of the market. Being first on a new platform can make or break a company. That doesn't mean you should jump on every single new platform that comes out, but you should at least have a look at what it would mean to be successful on a new platform.

Tim Ferris used this type of testing to get the title of his book figured out. He took out AdWords ads and tested the title options he had. He figured that the title and subtitle with the most email subscriptions was the best one to go with.

You can do the same thing with your idea and a landing page. There are numerous landing page services like Unbounce and Lead-Pages that will let you take email registrations without needing a whole site behind it. Many email providers do the same thing. I used the built in MailChimp landing pages for The Art of Focus and collected a few hundred emails.

If you want to get really specific, you could find out that one way of talking about the problem works best with the Instagram crowd and a different way works the best with Facebook ads. You can leverage this knowledge down the road as you do more marketing for your ideas.

One final word on ads, if at all possible pay only for conversions. Pay for sales or people on your email list, not just leads. This isn't always possible, but at least investigate what you're paying for. A confirmed lead is better than 20 eyeballs unless you're some big brand running a brand recognition campaign.

Speaking

If the idea you're planning to execute on is writing a book, you should know that the average author only makes around $40k a year. If you want to earn more than that, you will need to look at coaching and speaking.

Speaking in particular works because if you're up on a stage people view you as an authority. The first book I ever published was published the week after I spoke at a large conference in Vancouver BC. I spoke on the outline of the content from my book. Out of that I gained two coaching clients, and lots of book sales.

One of those coaching clients is still with me today so that speech has earned me over $20k in a few years. Speaking is worth it to establish yourself as an authority.

As with many of the other methods, use the laddering up approach here. Start with the local Meetups and community groups in your area. Most of them are hungry for anyone to speak. They're always looking to fill their speaking calendar.

You need to know how to build a good presentation if you want to be a good speaker. Look to Toastmasters as a way to get experience here. Also you need to read The Compelling Communicator because it will show you how to build a memorable presentation.

Yes, you're going to need to put in some work to be a good speaker, but the payoff is tremendous.

Networking/Meetups

When I read about networking and meetups, I admit that I cringe a bit inside. I'd say that I'm an introvert, but not in the way where you don't like to talk to people at all ever. I very much enjoy a good conversation with others. I take a walking meeting with someone almost every Friday afternoon, and those are some of the most valuable conversations I have every week.

Networking events, are exhausting and while I feel like I put so much effort in, I see little in the way of results. Even many conferences I head home early from the networking portion because I'm so tired after about 20 minutes of networking that I can't even think straight.

Instead I always try to grab three or four people that I want to connect with and head out to some restaurant. At a recent conference I grabbed 4 guys I know and wanted to know better. We had a wide ranging talk on family, business, finances, and being a good husband. That was the networking that I left and enjoyed.

Contrast that with my friend Sam. He heads out to a networking event and at the end has three business deals landed. He knows the names of almost everyone. He has people lined up to call him in the week to talk further.

Networking events can be great, but remember to stick with what you're good at.

If you're going to head out to a networking event, then you need to stand in the right spot to get good interactions. In her book Captivate, Vanessa Van Edwards, tells us that this is not at the door, and not by the food. By the door people will be looking over your head to see who else is there that is worth talking to. By the food, you're in the way of the food, move.

She says you should stand in what she calls the social zone. This is just after the food. If there are a set of tables, then it's probably there. If there are some couches, they're probably in the social zone. Here people are settled and ready to dig in to a conversation with you.

Don't lead in with the lame questions we've all been asked at an event like "What do you do?". Start with something that's memorable like, "What was the best thing that happened to you today?". Remember to speak more than you listen and as Dale Carnegie says:

> You can make more friends in two months by becoming interested in other people than you can in two years by trying to get other people interested in you. - How to Win Friends and Influence People

I remind myself before any networking event that I go to that to be interesting, I need to be interested in others. Spend time asking them more questions about what they do. Dig deeper in to any interest they have. Don't just wait for your turn to speak.

One final caution, is that you are not a business card machine gun. At one event, in the middle of a good conversation with a small group we had another guy walk up to interrupt with the question "do you have pets". It had nothing to do with the topic of discussion. He asked the question over the heads of a shorter person in the group. It was plain rude.

When some of us affirmed in a dazed manner that we did have pets he fired business cards into our hands and said something about his training business and then walked away. Into the silence I laughed, tossed the business card on the table that was full of random dishes and said "Is anyone really going to call that number?". No one was and they all laughed and followed my lead tossing the business card in to a pile of dishes.

You can't just head to a networking event to fire business cards at people. Go to meet interesting people and find out what they do. Connect them to others if you can. If it works that what you offer is something they need, tell them about it and invite them to talk to you another time. Grab their card then and ask about the best time to follow up. Write that on the back of the card along with some information about them. Then get back to being interested in the rest of their life outside of business.

PR and Unconventional PR

There are two types of PR. One is where you pitch your idea to different publications in your target industry. This could be websites or newspapers or magazines. Use the ladder up approach here. It's much more likely that your local newspaper will write a piece on you and your new business than a large national paper. It's much more likely that a small niche site will write about you than the biggest juggernaut in your field.

Many of these publications are looking for decent stories to fill their pages. You can be doing them a favour to give them a story worth telling. That does mean you need one worth telling though. If I was pitching my local paper about my story I'd be talking about how we focus so much on business success to the exclusion of success at home. We go to courses on management and sales, but when was the last time you went to a course on how to be a better spouse?

That's a story worth telling. Saying that I'm a business coach, is a dime a dozen story. It's not interesting in any fashion. I'm not nearly as interesting as I think. You're way more in love with your idea than everyone else is as well.

Another tack to take is some sort of PR stunt. You see Richard Branson doing PR stunts for many of his brands. He's dressed up as a bride, run a tank through Times Square, jumped off a building, tried to set a record with a hot air balloon flight around the world, and many other things.

Tesla recently did this as they launched a car in to space and gave you a live video feed of a dummy sitting in the car looking at whatever was out there in space.

Now those are big PR stunts, and out of reach of most companies as they get started. You don't have to do some huge stunt to get noticed.

Back when LESS Accounting was starting, they couldn't afford a booth at a conference. They were on a budget. What they could afford was a free lunch for people so they bought a bunch of food and went across the street to serve lunch.

They took to Twitter to tell the conference attendees that there was food across the street and that they should come over for a good meal. This brought in their target market and was memorable for the audacity of "stealing" the conference without actually being at the conference.

What could you do that would leverage something that's already going on? How can you be memorable?

Code and Engineering

Code and Engineering is about building something for your target prospects. This doesn't have to be a product, which we've already talked about. This can be something free like CoSchedule's free blog post headline analyzer.

To use it you need to put in your email address so you can get on their list. I use it regularly for my blog posts and I gave them my email for that privilege.

I'm starting to map out what a budgeting and lead acquisition calculator would look like. It would let you put in the income you want to earn and then tell you how much you needed to make revenue wise to make that happen. It would also let you say how much a project is worth and how many leads you land as projects. Then it would give you a weekly number to hit for the qualified leads you need to talk to if you want to hit your budget for the year.

While it's likely that my idea will have some sort of code written for it, you don't need that. My friend Adam has an investment calculator on his site that we set up in a Google Sheet on his site. You can see it on tuckinvesting.ca under the Joint Venture Real Estate navigation item.

He's not a particularly computer savvy and he built the sheet. My wife helped him get it on his site properly when she set up his website for him. Now he doesn't collect an email address for it at this point, but he could quite easily add that as a condition to use his investment calculator.

You would be surprised at the complex things you can build with a few WordPress plugins and some time spent configuring them. When you think of Code and Engineering, don't get stuck thinking about the actual code. Ask yourself, what do you want to deliver to your leads? Then see what it around that might do it for you already.

Other options

This book is not for startups flush with cash, so there are a bunch of things that I'm not going in to. They're expensive and I don't think they'll have the effect you need as someone trying to get their idea off the ground. I'll mention them below but we won't go into detail.

One area that is untapped by many people in the technology field is offline ads. That's TV, billboards, radio, and the local newspaper. For startups, these can be relatively inexpensive ways to build awareness of your brand and bring in curious customers. They are scatter shot though.

If you have a bit of a presence you can use affiliate marketing to get others bringing sales in to your pipeline. If you're running a WordPress site then using AffiliateWP is an inexpensive way to own your affiliate traffic and relationship as well. If you're just starting to see if your idea will land decently in the market, you're probably not ready for affiliate marketing though.

When you do try affiliate marketing, make sure you set a high bar for the affiliates you let in to your program. It's very easy to come across as sleazy if you're not careful. You can build a whole bunch of negative brand sentiment with a few bad affiliate marketers and you'll have to field a bunch of refunds. That management is going to kill you.

You've got a bunch of traction tools in your toolbox. You can test them out and see which ones fit your business the best. The biggest problem I see here is that so many people get just a bit of traction and then they want to jump in to the new thing with abandon.

I've done this, and it can hurt. The next chapter is all about how to build a smooth transition so that you don't end up where I did when I first tried to turn my coaching business in to my main work. It was a dark time, and without the supports I had in place, you may have never got to read this book.

13

STOP BURNING BRIDGES, BUILD A SMOOTH TRANSITION

I t's time for a bit of a confession, I'm a bridge burner. I see the new thing that I want to do and most of the stuff behind me is dead in my eyes. I did this with my web development business as I moved to coaching. I got some coaching students and sold some books and then just stopped caring about my web development business.

I didn't serve my current clients well. I didn't do any marketing or brand building on my web business. I paid the price in income and it was a big price.

I halved my income in a year!

While one year in to building the coaching and writing business was so much more successful than the first year of my web development business, it wasn't near as successful as my 10 year old web development firm. The money equation was also different because my wife was no longer working and we now have three kids.

Kids that want to do swimming lessons and camp and figure skating. Kids that need new clothes. Kids that want to play in big boxes as forts, not look at them as viable shelters from the rain.

I don't wish this type of transition on you. It's hard financially and hard on your relationships. The financial stress on top of building a business and trying to keep a relationship healthy can make any part of those things collapse in to failure.

Don't do what I started with. Use the process below to make a better plan to move from where you're at to where you want to be.

Keeping Your Spouse/Partner on Board

The first step in building a solid transition is to make sure that your spouse/partner is on board. When I first built my web development business my wife and I decided that for 6 months she'd do 99% of the work around the house. We'd get home from work and she'd make dinner while I went up to the spare room and worked on web stuff.

She did the dishes after I dashed down to eat. She cleaned the house and did the laundry while I worked on the weekends.

The deal was at the end of 6 months we'd evaluate where we were at. For me the end of 6 months was 4 clients in the pipeline for a total of $30k work with deposits in. I had 6 months of savings in the account to float a dry time and 5 solid leads that each were between 2-5k projects.

I quit my job and we went back to an even division of the chores around the house. I didn't just keep all the extra work time and leave her doing everything. We did not let that become the new normal, unlike so many freelancer's I've talked to.

As you look at your new idea, you need to sit down with your spouse/partner and figure out what a transition looks like for you. Remember at the beginning of the book, you should have done your filter documents on your own, and then together. You should already understand what each other value.

The plan to transition to your new field should not be a surprise. Your spouse should know about it. This is just the time where you work out the specifics of what it will look like for you and your family.

Your Time and Contribution

One of the first things to negotiate is what your contribution around the house and with income will be for the next period of time. I suggest that you start with three months. That's enough time to dig in to your goals and make some progress, without being so long that it's a wasteland of extra work for everyone.

It's important for you both to recognize that while you may have earned your way out of evenings and weekend work with your main job, you aren't there yet as you launch you new idea. To launch my writing and coaching business, I wrote in the evenings or scheduled emails to send the next morning. I did reading and research on the couch with my wife.

I occasionally woke up extra early on the weekend and worked till 9am so that I could hit my weekly writing totals.

No, I did not enjoy working evenings and weekends. I didn't like the extra time away from my kids. The thing is, if I wanted to launch the new business that's what it took so I did the extra work.

My wife took on a few extra house chores, and would take the kids out to the splash park so I could write for an extra hour or two. She agreed that changing my income stream from web development clients to coaching and writing was a net win for our family, so she sacrificed right alongside me to make it happen.

I would not have had either successful business without my wife.

In the midst of this, we still blocked off times that we hung out as a family. Friday night is family pizza night. I'd be done work by around 4pm and help make pizza. Saturday afternoons were family time. We'd hike or take the kids to the splash park, where I admit sometimes I'd do some more research for my writing. Even when I was researching, the priority was family so if the kids came up for some attention I'd put my research down and head off to watch whatever bug or leaf they wanted to show me.

We also saved all of Sunday. First, my wife would run in the mornings, then we'd head to church and the afternoon was for whatever we decided to do. In the hot days of summer as I finished this book, it was for laying around at the river while the kids played and the adults napped and swam when they felt too hot.

When I launched my web development business I had more time to work on the weekends because we didn't have kids and my wife worked retail. I could work as much as I wanted on Saturday because she was gone all day. Then we saved Friday night and Sunday for time for us to do stuff together.

You and your family need to work out what will happen with your time around the house. Even more importantly you need to put a time limit on it. Far to many people start "hustling" and then years later realize that it's all hustle.

When we had our second child we wanted me to take a month off work. That meant I worked an extra three hours a day from September to December 21. Then I was off until February 15th. We had our second daughter on January 27th and I had time to hang out with her and support my wife and our oldest child as we figured out what it meant to have two kids.

Don't be the idea person that makes hustle the new normal. Stick to that time limit and meet every three months to figure out what work and life will look like for the next three months. Keep making the deal work for your family every three months so that you don't look back with a successful business and broken relationships.

Savings and Income

One of the next things you need to decide together is what will your finances look like through the transition. Are you willing to move back down in income for a period of time before the new idea/business gets the traction it needs? How much less are you willing to earn and for how long?

You should already know what your basic income is, and what your dream income is. If you don't head back to Part I of the book and do the work together. You need to decide together what you can live on.

If you're looking to leave a job and do something on your own, you'll need some savings. Do you need three months saved or six months? If you and your spouse disagree on the amount that needs to be saved, you should always go with the most conservative person unless it's unreasonable.

Unreasonable is you saying that you need six months and your spouse saying that you need 24 months saved. There is likely some other issue going on that you need to deal with. If you say six months and they say nine months, go with nine.

If they are asking for something that seems unreasonable to you, it's not time to get angry, it's time to dig deeper. I had one coaching client that didn't get the support he needed from his spouse. She just wasn't in to any of his ideas at all and wasn't afraid to say it.

Once I had a chance to talk to her I found out that this was the fifth idea he had. The other four he never really talked to her about, he just started doing them. With idea three, he quit his job and just sort of didn't mention it. He got dressed like he was going to work and went to the coffee shop to "work" on his new idea.

Needless to say, there was little trust and he had to take it really slow. She was willing to admit that she thought he could do amazing things, and that this was the first time he had hired a coach to help with a transition so he seemed much more serious about it, but she needed a bunch more trust built up before she was willing to take any risk at all.

We ended up with Saturday from 6am - 12pm where he'd head off and do the work needed to launch his idea. That was the only sacrifice she was willing to make in the first three months. At the end of three months when his main income hadn't dropped at all and he was seeing some traction with the new business, she was ready to buy in to the idea more.

You can't win at your work while fighting a battle at home especially if you're trying to launch something new. Take the time to work out a transition plan that your spouse is comfortable with. If it takes you an extra year to make the transition, but you keep your marriage, it's worth the extra year.

Reporting

One key step in making the transition smooth with your spouse is doing regular reports on how things are going. For my transition from web development to writing and coaching that meant that I'd report on how many web clients I had. How many leads were in the pipeline and the approximate value I expected from the leads that would land.

It also meant I reported on the number of coaching clients I had and what types of leads were on that side. It meant I told her about the books I had in the queue and any other writing contracts I had. We talked about what marketing channels I was using and how they were performing.

We'd do a weekly recap of where things were at and then a monthly bigger planning thinking session on the two businesses. I'm very lucky that my wife reads lots of business books. She's invested in improving herself. She was willing to dig in to the business and my fears with it and help me work through it.

If you don't have that, you still should be doing your best to provide your spouse/partner with an update on how things are going in the business. If they're not willing to dig deep, make sure you have an accountability partner that's a few steps ahead of you or on the same journey.

Don't get stuck with someone that only says they want to build something new but never does any work. Make sure you are accountable with someone that is taking measurable steps towards their goal. Someone that won't take your crap and will hold your feet to the fire.

You might be able to do it on your own, but it's going to be a much harder and longer road to walk if you're going to do it by yourself.

Don't Burn The Boats

I've said it already, I'm absolutely a boat burner. Once I've moved on to the "new" thing that is exciting, I have to fight to put any time in to whatever is currently supporting me and my family. Case in point was putting almost no effort in to my web development business. No marketing, and maybe 50% of my effort was in to the web business. Not even a good 50%, just a passable 50%.

This abrupt focus change harmed our families finances. It put strain on my marriage. I made poor decisions about how I parented because I was stressed out by the lack of funds.

I made some of my web clients angry because I didn't deliver the work on time.

Don't burn the boats behind you as much as you may want to. Instead, take a measured approach to changing your business focus.

Running Two Businesses

First, it's hard to run two different businesses. Even if you're only putting a barely passable 50% in to one business like I was, it's hard to keep that much going.

This is a good thing because it's going to force you to only do the things that bring the most value in your work. For my web development business, after some financial pain, it forced me to realize that the only service I should be offering is a quick setup of your Membership site. No custom code, just set up your stuff for you.

Don't plan on running two businesses forever. You won't be able to maintain the energy. You'll resent the "old" thing and thus short-change it. The longer you do the "old" thing while wanting to transition to the new idea the more you'll resent how you keep getting pulled away from what you would rather be doing.

Block Your Time

You should already know your basic income levels. You should know what you need to bring in per month to pay the bills, then what higher amount makes life feel comfortable. Before you embark on building out your new thing, you need to streamline your business so that it can bring in the income you need in as little time as possible.

While I could charge big bucks for custom development, it could also take much longer than anticipated. I could sit there for a whole day without figuring out why my code wasn't working. This is not something that is suited to running an efficient business which is why I started doing the site setups.

By focusing on those less technical projects I could give customers a two week window for their project. Week one I would set the whole thing up and in week two they could report any issues and have access to me for any questions.

There were not big issues in this that took days to figure out, and I had the support teams of the tools I was using behind me to answer any questions because I was using their tools out of the box. I could put aside the time it took to setup a site and know that I'd hit that time with 99% accuracy.

Like I said, I'm a boat burner, so I had to set this system up after I experienced the pain of loss of income. I had to go backwards and set up marketing to support this part of my business. Don't be like me, set it up first so that you can start to make your transition and not have to stop and backtrack.

Once you have a standard offering, it's time to block out your days so that you can focus on the different things you have going in your work. I write in the mornings and focus on my coaching and writing business then. In the afternoons I do site setups for clients.

I generally start at 6am and write until 9am. Then I take a 2 - 3 hour break. During this break I run or hang out with my kids. Then from 12 - 3pm I work for clients.

Some days when I have a bit more that needs to get done I might edit podcasts or do something else that doesn't take a lot of brain power after 3pm, but most days I just finish up the day.

Note, that to do this I make sure that I'm using all of the focus tips I provided in Part II. You can't expect to be scattered and distracted like regular people and be able to keep this going. If you let distraction creep in, then get ready to fail in your endeavours.

Do You Keep Going?

We start our new ideas and businesses with all the hope in the world. Nothing can stop us. We dream big and figure that if only a small percentage of our target market thinks we have something to offer we will be swimming in our Scrooge McDuck money pit.

Unfortunately, that rarely happens. Oh we think it happens more than it does because news sites and social media sensationalize the few that make it in this manner. They're showing off the 1 in 10,000 that make it. The other 9,999 are wondering when if ever they're going to get any traction.

In The Dip, Seth Godin provides us with three great questions to ask ourselves when we are in this situation. It's the ones I've turned back to when I have been struggling with my own inadequacy in the midst of an idea that isn't getting traction as fast as I hoped.

Am I Panicking

Godin's first question is "Am I Panicking." It's easy to panic because when we started this endeavour we dreamed what we thought were small dreams. We figured on a market of millions and if only 1% of those millions purchased from us, we'd have it made.

Well we're not seeing that traction. We're not seeing the market of millions. We're currently seeing a market of hundreds and they mostly don't care about what we have to say.

Next thing you know we're thinking that our idea and our knowledge is probably useless. We start eyeing that box our kids are playing with and wondering how good it will do when we have to move in to it down by the river.

If you've planned your transition well, and not burned the boats like I did, then you should still have income taken care of. If you didn't plan well, then it's time to backtrack and make sure that you have taken care of your income properly.

It's important not to let some in the moment event turn you into the panic monster. Keep working the plan you came up with. Keep working with your mentor or mastermind group. Take their suggestions and test them out for your business.

Who Am I Trying to Influence

Most times it's not that your idea is terrible, at least if you've ranked it and done the research I've talked about. You have an idea, but you're either not presenting it properly or not enough people know about you. In fact most times most of your target market has no idea that you even exist.

You have a few more questions to ask yourself as you look at who you are trying to influence. First, do you have the career capital to further the idea you're talking about? You should have already put some thought in to this, but ask yourself again now.

What would it take to have the career capital to make this fly? What would your content/blog/idea need to look like to get more people interested?

It's also worth looking back at your strategies for traction again. Did you honestly go through each one and give it a proper effort? Did you ignore one because of some self-held bias? Who can you ask to help you see that bias so you can get it out of your work?

You have a good idea! You need to keep testing how to expose it to more people so that you can expand your market.

Is There Any Measurable Progress?

Finally, what measurable progress is there? When I wasn't seeing my coaching business taking off, I was seeing a bunch of measurable progress. I was getting offered more paid writing gigs that would help freelancers.

I was getting email replies saying that my blog posts and ideas were amazing and changing people's businesses.

I was adding some people to my coaching programs, just not enough.

I continued to see opportunities come up that would help me get my ideas further. While it was discouraging that none of them were the rocket launch of success I was hoping for, they were all little affirmations that I was on the right path.

What type of progress have you made in the last few months? Have you had clients say they love working with you? Have you had a few people love your idea?

While we dream of rocket ship style growth, most growth is slow and steady. A few steps forward and a few steps back. It's frustrating to live in that place. It can be a struggle to pay the bills, but that is where you sit if you want to do something that matters.

Note the little pieces of affirmation that happen and cling to them as you keep going.

More Side Than Hustle

For some ideas and people, it is time to stop putting so much focus on them. I had to take my coaching business back to more side than hustle because it wasn't bringing in the income I wanted.

I had to reevaluate my priorities and look at what brought in the most income for a minute of effort. I had to start talking more about doing WordPress Membership sites and less about coaching.

I had to stop blogging daily, and publishing 70k words a month, because while I was seeing more and more traction, I wasn't yet seeing income.

Yes this was disappointing, but it was also a fabulous constraint. Knowing I had to spend less time on coaching meant that I could only ever do the few small items that brought the most impact. I cut all the linking and short blog posts, because they were the least helpful to my readers. While they didn't take up hours of time individually, cumulatively over a week they did add up to a few hours.

I had to cut back my book podcast, Should I Read It, from two episodes a week to a single episode a week so that I could cut some reading time and still keep up with a new book review every other week. I had to put it on hold for a few weeks to push on some other marketing tasks.

I put more time back in to marketing my development business and streamlined it so that it was maximally efficient. I learned a lot in this process, and that's what I've been sharing with you because it worked for me.

I was able to head back to coaching like I wanted and still have the income that my family needed.

Don't Go It Alone

We're coming to the end of the book here and the last thing I want to impress upon you is that you can't go it alone.

You should have your spouse/partner on your side already but even their support is probably not going to be enough. You're going to need people around you to help you when things suck.

I needed people around me in the darkest times of my business because I was at least wondering if my family would have an easier time financially if I was dead. I thought about this sometimes when I was up in the mountains hiking something on a Saturday morning.

I was so tired of the financial struggle. The stress at home due to money being so tight. I was so so tired of wondering how I'd pay us twice a month. At times it felt like the best thing would be to have some sort of accident when I was on a mountain. Then insurance would take care of my family financially and in the mountains slips and mistakes happen.

Those are scary times, because even though I knew that my wife would not be better off without me and that my kids would miss me, it still was at least a viable option. It felt easier than continuing the struggle to get noticed.

Masterminds

While I did not open up in my mastermind about the depths of my despair, I did talk a bunch about feeling like a fraud. I was saying that you could run a great business and still see your kids while I was struggling to make that happen for me.

It was in my mastermind group that I got more affirmation that I was on the right path. Where I heard that I had helped someone in the group make the same transition I was making. Where I heard that I helped someone double their revenue in a single year.

You can't go it alone, and a mastermind is one of the best things that you can have around to help you. Well run mastermind groups will help you generate new ideas for your business. They'll give you kick in the pants when you need motivation, and come alongside you when you need some support.

In one of the mastermind groups I ran another participant emailed their 30,000 strong list about a book I released. At the time my email list was 200 people, so the effect was huge. From a trickle of sales it turned into a few hundred sales.

From a few people talking to me about coaching, I had 20 interested. My friend Justin graciously spent some of his career capital on me because he trusted me.

All it takes to run a mastermind group is a few people willing to care as much about your business as their business. You should be meeting at least every other week. I've heard of monthly groups, but in my experience you never really get the pulse of the other businesses.

Some groups use a "hotseat" model where someone is the focus for the day. Others mention big rocks they have going on at the end, but you spend most of the time focusing on a single person and their business.

Others run a weekly accountability style. You show up talking about what went well, what didn't, how you're going to fix any issues so they don't block you next week. Then you usually end with the goals for the next week.

The later format is what I use for the mastermind groups that I run. If you need some accountability and support, make sure you reach out to see if you're a good fit.

Coaching

After mastermind groups, you can get more focused attention if you pay for coaching. I offer this to freelancer fathers that want to stream-line their business so that they can be the dad they've always dreamed of.

One of my students took his development business and turned it from custom development in to a retainer only productized service. He cut the hours he worked and increased his revenue.

He was able to do this because I helped hold him accountable and told him when his ideas were bad. I asked him a bunch of hard questions about what his business was looking like, about how he'd implement the new parts of his business he was thinking of.

I'm not the right coach for everyone, but there is someone out there that fits exactly what you need. Take some time to look through the books you loved and the blogs that you always turn to for advice. See if they offer any coaching and then test it out to see if it's for you.

You can run so much further faster if you have someone on your side making you dig deeper than you can on your own.

Friends

This is where I opened up about the struggles I was having as I hiked. These were the men that I told about at least entertaining no longer being around.

In The Happiness Advantage, Shawn Achor shows us that the people that get through the darkest times at work and at home had a strong network of friends around them. Friends that would show up and be a shoulder to lean on when things were tough.

If I didn't have my friends to lean on, you may never have read this book. You may have read about me in the local newspaper as some tragic accident on a mountain, but you wouldn't be reading this book.

It takes courage to be honest with those around you. You may need to take the first step and be vulnerable with people that you have never been vulnerable with before.

The support is worth it. If you're going to embark on building the life you want without ruining your relationships, then things will get hard and you will need help to keep going.

Make sure you have people around you that care about you and can help. It's scary to open up about the hard things you're going through, but it's freeing in so many ways. I was lucky because talking about my thoughts of suicide a few times helped me see the faulty logic I was using.

I lucked in to fairly fast freedom from these thoughts.

Awesome File

The final way that I don't go it alone is by having an awesome file. This is a filed copy of all the awesome things that people have said about me.

The emails I get when something I wrote helped someone. Stories of the people I helped earn an extra few thousand dollars on their contracts which meant they didn't need to work weekends to make ends meet anymore.

I keep mine in a piece of software, but you can just a jar or a file folder. Just have something to remind you of all the ways you've helped people when things are hard and you want to stop moving forward.

During my dark times when I was wondering how much easier it would be if I wasn't around, I went to that file every day. Sometimes multiple times a day, to make sure that I remembered I was helping people with all the work I was doing. Maybe I wasn't seeing the income comparable to the help I was providing, but it would come if I kept travelling down the path I was on.

AFTERWORD

That's all I've got to say about that. Over the course of The Art of Focus I've walked you through three main areas.

First, we looked at building out some filtering documents and ideas for what we want to do. We ran our ideas through our filtering documents because no one wants to build a life they hate.

Second, we looked at what focus means. What types of actions and attitude do you need to have to achieve success? If you don't take control of your time and be effective with every minute you're "working" then it's going to be hard to get anything worthwhile done.

Finally, we looked at what it takes to start getting traction with your ideas. I showed you the process I use to research ideas and then test traction channels to see which one is best suited.

We finished off the last section with a serious discussion about getting help when you're struggling. You can't go it alone. You're not alone.

The rest is up to you. What are you going to do with the information you've learned? Did you do all the work? Have you had the conversations you needed to with your spouse to get on the same page?

It's time for you to take action and start building focus in to your life so that you can build the life you've been wanting for so long.

DON'T MISS THIS!

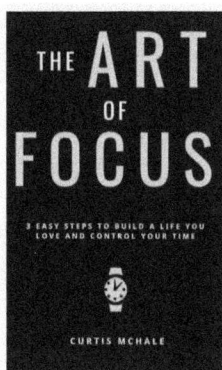

If you like videos, make sure you sign up for my email list at curtismchale.ca/recommends/focus-email. You'll get that free audio copy of my book and access to the first module of my 8 Week Business BootCamp.

The first module is all about Part I of the book. You'll hear me walk you through your filtering documents and provide you with a stack of questions you can use to build out your documents.

You'll also get the **FREE** companion workbook for this book and access to the **FREE** audiobook.

THANKS

Thank You For Reading My Book!

I appreciate all the feedback I receive on my books. I want to be the best writing I can be and most importantly, **I want to provide you with helpful actionable advice.**

I need your input to do that. Please leave me a helpful review on Amazon so I can make my next book even better than this one.

Thanks and have an awesome day!
— Curtis McHale

9 7 8 1 7 7 5 3 3 6 4 3 3